Teaching materials for disadvantaged children

Report of the Schools Council Project on the
Use of Project Materials by Teachers of
Disadvantaged Pupils in Secondary Schools,
based at the School of Education, University
of Birmingham

Ronald Gulliford
and Paul Widlake

Evans/Methuen Educational

First published 1975 for the Schools Council
by Evans Brothers Limited
Montague House, Russell Square, London WC1B 5BX
and Methuen Educational Limited
11 New Fetter Lane, London EC4P 4EE

Distributed in the U S by Citation Press
Scholastic Magazines Inc., 50 West 44th Street
New York, NY 10036
and in Canada by Scholastic–T A B Publications Ltd
123 Newkirk Road
Richmond Hill, Ontario

ISBN 0 423 89110 3

Printed in Great Britain by
Richard Clay (The Chaucer Press) Ltd
Bungay, Suffolk

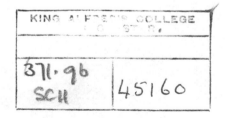

Contents

Foreword

In 1972 the Schools Council set up a one-year project (under the directorship of Ronald Gulliford at the School of Education, University of Birmingham, with Paul Widlake as research officer) to examine the use of project materials by teachers of disadvantaged children. The project was the outcome of one of the recommendations in Schools Council Working Paper 27, *'Cross'd with Adversity': the Education of Socially Disadvantaged Children in Secondary Schools* (Evans/Methuen Educational, 1970). It was felt that the least successful fifteen to twenty per cent of the school population might not be benefiting from the wider range of curriculum opportunities which development work was creating. The project at Birmingham was established to examine the problems of pupils with learning difficulties in using existing project materials, to consider ways in which materials have been used with disadvantaged children, or adapted by teachers and project teams to make them suitable, and to make successful adaptations more widely known.

The project obtained information from a considerable number of LEAs. The report is based on information from schools about their experience of using a variety of project materials in language, the humanities, social and moral education, science and mathematics. Most of the projects considered are Schools Council projects, but some are projects set up by the Nuffield Foundation, or local education authorities, and one, a project set up privately. In some instances only the trial materials were available at the time of the survey and, where possible, details of the final published materials have been included, or brought up to date.

It is hoped that this survey of current practice and successful adaptation in the use of project materials with disadvantaged children will be a useful source of reference for teachers, and that the recommendations for future development in this field will be of interest to all those concerned in the education of these children.

Acknowledgements

We should like to acknowledge with gratitude the co-operation and help of the directors of Schools Council projects and their project teams who willingly gave us so much help in undertaking this inquiry.

We should also like to thank the directors of education who replied to our initial inquiry and the many teachers who sent in helpful information and comments as well as receiving us on visits to their schools.

We are also grateful for the help given by the members of the project consultative committee, by Miss Helen Carter of the Schools Council at various stages in the project, and by Mrs Dorothy Bennett who undertook so willingly and efficiently all the secretarial work which the project and its report has entailed.

Part I

The purpose of the survey: its conclusions and recommendations

I. The purpose and nature of the survey

How to give the best educational help to backward and disadvantaged pupils in secondary schools is a question to which there are, as yet, no firm answers. Should these children be taught in remedial classes or streams or should they be included in mixed ability groups and be withdrawn for special help in some subjects? How far can they (or should they) follow courses provided for the average range of pupils? Do they need curricula planned specially for them? How far are they benefiting from recent curriculum developments, and from new techniques of presenting information and of instruction? There has been insufficient discussion of such questions. Indeed, as was shown in the Department of Education and Science report, *Slow Learners in Secondary Schools*,* special help for slow-learning and disadvantaged children has been unevenly provided and has often been seriously inadequate.

This report is concerned with one aspect of this topic. An inquiry was undertaken at the request of the Schools Council into the use, with the least successful children, of curricula and materials developed by Schools Council and other projects. Were these materials and fresh ideas in curricula only being used with average and successful pupils or were they reaching the least successful pupils? If they were used with the least successful pupils, were they suitable for these children? To what extent did teachers need to adapt materials or modify methods of teaching? The terms of reference were as follows:

a   To examine the problems experienced by a broad spectrum of pupils with learning difficulties – both the under-achieving and slow learners – when using existing materials produced by certain Schools Council projects, with a view to isolating the particular difficulties caused by the materials as originally presented.

b   To consider ways in which materials have been used – or adapted – by teachers and by project teams to make them accessible to pupils at the lower end of the ability range, with a view to examining the principles upon which successful uses and adaptations have been based.

* Education Survey 15 (HMSO, 1971).

9

c   To publish a survey of good practice, including descriptions of particularly successful adaptations, which would, among other things, attempt to consider the factors essential to the successful use of materials with pupils at the lower end of the ability range and, in particular, with limited linguistic resources.

Defining disadvantaged pupils

It was necessary first of all to consider what pupils the project was concerned with. It was convenient to refer to the group as the 15 to 20 per cent of pupils who were the least successful in school. This would include pupils in remedial classes and the lower streams of secondary schools and pupils in special schools. It was recognized that many of these children would be found in groups of mixed ability. Teachers in schools and the staff of projects knew, in general terms, which children we were concerned with, referring to them variously as slow learners, remedial or disadvantaged children, but the reports quoted later in the survey do not distinguish clearly between different kinds of problem.

The least successful 20 per cent of pupils includes, of course, a variety of kinds of educational failure. Schools vary both in the proportion of these and in the extent to which they provide for them. Some pupils make poor progress mainly because of limited ability and this is usually combined with other factors. Others make very poor progress in spite of average – perhaps even above-average – ability. Among these, we should distinguish first those whose difficulty with general school work is due to underlying difficulties in acquiring basic skills of reading, writing and mathematics, though they may be competent in other ways and fairly normal in their general adjustment. Secondly, we should distinguish those whose poor response to schooling is related to adverse environmental circumstances which have denied them the security and emotional adjustment essential for consistent application to the tasks of learning. These are pupils who are liable to have behaviour difficulties, to be more frequently absent and to have negative attitudes to school and achievement. Though not unintelligent, they may function at a low level owing to a limited background of language and experiences in their home environments. In explaining the purposes of the inquiry, we have always been careful to point out that we were not just concerned with slow learners but also with disadvantaged children in this sense. In addition, we have included children from overseas whose language difficulties and cultural differences make for poor progress in school. In practice, of course, these groups overlap. Individual children are unsuccessful for a combination of personal and environmental reasons.

Although we may distinguish between these different kinds of educational

10

failure, it is probably more useful to delineate the group of children we are concerned with by referring to certain common characteristics which may necessitate modification of the content of materials and methods of instruction.

Low achievement in basic skills

Backwardness in reading means that many textbooks, work sheets and resource materials cannot easily be used. Deficiencies in spelling, handwriting and written expression are a serious limitation on ways of consolidating and evaluating learning.

Limitations of language

Even when reading levels are adequate, there may be difficulty in fully comprehending the language and the concepts used in books and other materials, or generally in classroom communication. Talking about ideas, asking questions and discussing are forms of language use to which these children are often relatively unaccustomed.

Limitations of understanding

Limited ability and lack of experience often result in pupils not being ready for thinking about abstract ideas and principles or for logical thought in explaining and interpreting. Even in practical activities, they may need help to observe relevantly and to focus on the essentials. There is a wide range of ability in these respects. Some disadvantaged pupils are very immature in their thinking, while others surprise with their grasp of ideas – even though they may have difficulty in communicating them orally and in writing.

Limited interest in learning and weak desire for achievement

Not surprisingly, pupils who are not very successful are liable to show less interest in school work, to be less eager to achieve – some tend towards apathy, others towards anti-school attitudes. Long experience of failure, lack of encouragement from home and poor concentration and ability to persevere may make it difficult to arouse interest and stimulate effort in these children. It should be said, of course, that much depends on the suitability of work and expectations at school, on relationships with the teacher and the general attitude of the school towards backward children. Many schools have found ways of minimizing negative feelings by planning appropriate curricula and by methods of organization which promote acceptance and involvement.

11

Difficult behaviour

Educational failure is likely to have behaviour problems as by-products – either some degree of awkward, aggressive behaviour or (as serious a problem in group work and discussion) withdrawal and non-participation. In addition, children from unsettled or unstable backgrounds are obviously more likely to present discipline problems which interfere with the smooth organization of a learning situation.

These characteristics help to delineate the group of children we were concerned with and indicate some of the reasons why this inquiry was needed.

Relevance of Schools Council and other projects to disadvantaged pupils

Another major consideration in undertaking this inquiry was to decide which projects were relevant to the needs of disadvantaged children. As suggested earlier, there is no clear consensus of opinion about the curricular needs of slow-learning and disadvantaged children. Some feel that there should be no radical difference in the courses for the least successful pupils – that they should have the opportunity for as wide an experience as possible and any differences should be in the methods of presentation and teaching. To do otherwise would tend towards segregation, making these children appear and feel different, as well as prematurely closing doors to educational opportunities. Others feel that the limitations of these pupils, and their personal and social needs, indicate a need for courses with less academic emphasis and a greater social and functional one.

We shall not discuss these issues here but limit ourselves to stating certain generalizations about the needs of disadvantaged children which we have had in mind in thinking about the curriculum.

First, there is the need of most disadvantaged children for the best possible help in acquiring and improving basic skills in literacy and communication. A number of projects in language contribute directly to this: in reading there is *Breakthrough to Literacy* and in language there are *Language in Use* and courses prepared for immigrant pupils. Materials prepared specially for the teaching of reading and communication tend to become quickly known and used and we have been rather more interested in the opportunities provided by courses in other curriculum areas (e.g. science, environmental studies, humanities) for improving basic skills. Learning and activity in these areas can create the need and desire to improve basic skills and provide the motivated practice for doing so. One reason we were glad to undertake this inquiry was our impression that, while remedial reading has received much attention, the possibilities of general curriculum studies in helping basic skills as well as pupils' general education

12

have been somewhat neglected. Evidence supporting this impression lies in the relative availability of reading books for backward readers compared with the great shortage of texts and materials suitable for slow learners in other aspects of the curriculum.

Secondly, the curriculum can be a means of compensating disadvantaged children for certain inadequacies and deprivations in their previous development and experience. Whereas in the past there was a tendency to see retarded thinking, language and communication as inevitable limitations on the scope and nature of the work expected of slow learners, we now tend to see a varied and stimulating curriculum as a means of developing and improving thinking and language skills. In this view, what and how much of the content of a course is learnt is less important than the process of learning – how far pupils have become better able to think and talk about ideas. This difference in emphasis is an important one for the specialist teacher working with slow learners. It was also important to us since we have not considered it necessary for disadvantaged children to be able to cover all of a proposed course. If a course contained topics and sequences of work relevant to slow learners and, moreover, was capable of furthering their capacity and desire to learn, we have considered it relevant to our inquiry.

The environment of disadvantaged children may be rich in certain kinds of experience, but it is a reasonable generalization that their horizons may be narrow, and they tend to be restricted in many kinds of experience which are often assumed in school work. Curricular activities which make the most of the immediate environment seem particularly valuable to them – geography and science which widen their awareness of the natural environment; humanities and social studies which draw attention to aspects of the community. It would be regrettable if project materials concerned with these curricular areas were not being used with disadvantaged children.

The teacher working with disadvantaged children is naturally involved in their personal development. Emotional immaturities, poor adjustment, delinquency, difficulties in relationships and social behaviour are often problems to be grappled with as a first step towards more normal educational progress and achievement. How far can the curriculum contribute to the amelioration of these problems? The curriculum contributes indirectly by providing opportunities for success, interest, enjoyment and new experience. Opportunities for personal expression through creative work, drama, discussion and personal writing are acknowledged to be important elements in a therapeutic approach. In addition, there is a need for work which aims directly to promote thought and awareness of moral issues, relationships and social behaviour generally. A number of projects in social and moral education seemed potentially valuable for this purpose.

13

We do not hold preconceived notions that certain subjects or topics are too difficult or inappropriate for slow-learning or disadvantaged children. One is so often surprised by the work which enthusiastic teachers have accomplished with such children. What is important, however, is the way in which topics are presented and how pupils are expected to learn. The crucial thing is to know the levels of thinking and understanding that pupils start from and to adapt the content, methods and pace of teaching accordingly. This, of course, was one of the main issues in our inquiry.

Methods of inquiry

The project was viewed as an exploratory one of a year's duration (from January to December 1972) and was undertaken by a part-time director and one full-time research associate.

A variety of methods were used in order to gain as much information as possible about the use of project materials with disadvantaged children.

Before the survey began, a letter was sent by the Schools Council to every local education authority in England and Wales to inform them of its purpose and ask them for details of schools using project materials. From the 163 LEAs, sixty-five replies were received, and information was sorted into lists of schools using particular projects. Information was added subsequently from other sources.

At the beginning of the survey, a letter was sent to the directors of relevant projects setting out at some length the purpose of the survey and asking for their co-operation in finding schools using their project materials with slow learners. At the same time, arrangements were made to visit project directors, to discuss with them and their staff the aims and nature of their projects, and to obtain at first hand their views about the use of their materials with slow learners and disadvantaged children. The staff of projects were most helpful and very interested in the subject of the inquiry. In most cases they were able to provide information about schools using their materials with disadvantaged children.

An important part of the research officer's work was to make himself acquainted as thoroughly as possible with teachers' guides, reports and articles related to each project. A number of these include references to the experience of teachers of disadvantaged children, and some projects' evaluation reports contained data relevant to our survey.

Other methods were used to cast the net as wide as possible and to maximize the chances of our hearing of relevant work with disadvantaged children. Mention was made of the survey in several journals, including *Remedial Education* and *Special Education*, and at a number of conferences and meetings of teachers in remedial and special education. Information and views were also sought

14

from relevant associations of specialist teachers and from tutors of full-time courses in remedial and special education.

In addition, every teachers' centre in the country was circularized in the hope of hearing of more schools using projects with slow learners or of making contact with working parties or groups of teachers meeting to discuss the curriculum for slow learners. At the same time, an offer was made to send to any centres with such groups a short outline of discussion topics related to the subject of our inquiry.

From all these sources, lists were drawn up of schools using particular projects. These schools (a total of one thousand) were invited to comment on their experience of using project materials. We did not consider it appropriate to ask schools to complete a very detailed questionnaire but we asked them to respond to a number of open-ended questions. This brought a considerable amount of information, and many schools wrote at some length. A few basic details about size of school, organization of work with slow learners, and the kind of population which the school drew on were included.

This information, together with the recommendations of project directors, was used to select schools for visiting. The short term of the project precluded a very extensive programme of visits but a sample of the schools was visited to obtain examples of work with each of the main projects studied in different parts of the country.

In the case of the Moral Education Project (13–16), it was possible to run a small experiment using some of the project's materials in a number of Midland secondary and special schools. Although this project appeared to be very suitable, there was only a little information available about its use with slow learners and disadvantaged children. Additionally, certain other materials were given short trials by a number of teachers, and in two cases special studies undertaken by teachers on one-year full-time courses were made available to us.

In summary, using a variety of means and drawing on a wide range of sources, it proved possible to gather sufficient information from which to derive some answers to the questions posed.

II. Some general conclusions

This chapter discusses some general issues about the use of Schools Council and other projects with disadvantaged children. Later chapters are concerned with projects in particular subject areas based on our examination of their relevance to disadvantaged children and on the experience of schools using them.

Although the number of projects to study and the short duration of the survey did not permit exhaustive inquiries, we were able to locate a number of schools making use of project materials with less successful pupils. Among these, some were doing so with considerable success and there were encouraging signs of progress in tackling the problem of introducing a wider curriculum to these children. At the same time, it must be recorded that, in spite of the efforts of the publishers and of the Schools Council in dissemination, the work of teachers' centres and other sources of in-service training, there seems often scant awareness of what various projects have to offer. Indeed, it may be that teachers of less successful pupils in remedial departments and special schools have assumed that project materials are not suitable.

From our examination of what Schools Council and other projects have to offer, we have been impressed with the range of ideas and materials which could contribute to the education of less successful pupils. We feel they go some way towards making good the lack of suitable materials which has often been commented on by teachers. Those of us who have been concerned with these pupils for a long time recall the period when the main problem was seen to be one of obtaining sufficiently simple reading books with content suitable for the maturity and interest levels of older pupils. The supply of these improved but the problem remained of finding suitable books in science, history, geography and mathematics. Teachers of specialist subjects have often been very uncertain how to provide for the less able pupils; remedial teachers have often been uncertain what advice to give their specialist colleagues. The difficulty has really been a fundamental one of confusion and uncertainty about the aims of education of the least successful pupils and about ways of organizing it. The Department of Education and Science report, *Slow Learners in Secondary Schools*,* which reports a survey of arrangements in 158 schools illustrates this. 'Uncertainty of aims and methods for the "slow learners" was immediately apparent in many – indeed in the majority of the schools visited . . . there is little evidence of any

* Education Survey 15 (HMSO, 1971).

16

attempt to discover the potential of these pupils.' On the one hand, the survey reported a tendency in some schools to confine the work to attempts to improve reading, writing and composition; and on the other hand, the report expresses unease about the exposure of slow learners to the full pattern of specialization and a common curriculum with the more able, with little differentiation between pupils except for a simpler approach, a slower pace and slight modifications to existing schemes of work for slow learners.

Another comment in this report was that 'little evidence exists of suitably planned and integrated courses adapted to the needs of slow learners and designed to discover their interests and develop their strengths.' While Schools Council and other projects do not in themselves provide a complete solution to this problem, we do hold the view that any teacher or team of teachers looking for ideas and materials to employ in the teaching of disadvantaged children would find the following a profitable source – materials from the science projects, Geography for the Young School Leaver, Mathematics for the Majority Continuation Project, the Moral Education Project (13–16), and also the work of the North West Regional Curriculum Development Project.

Projects which appear relevant or suitable will be considered in detail in Part 2. At this point, we propose to make a number of generalizations about these projects in terms of features which teachers consider important in teaching less successful pupils.

Need for practical experience and activity

A feature of all the projects studied is the emphasis given to learning based on the pupils' own activity and experiment, or which draws on their personal and environmental experience. While there are indeed many difficulties in carrying this through (it is much harder to organize than desk-bound, textbook-based learning), it is nevertheless a fact that the practical, active approach, long recognized as essential for the most educationally handicapped, is being advocated and practised with a larger proportion of the secondary-school population. In consequence, there is less of a gap between the methods of teaching being proposed for average pupils and that required by below-average pupils. The need for a radical difference in approach in teaching the 'backward' is less pronounced, though there must be differences in presentation and assessment. This fact is reflected in the number of reports we have received of pupils with quite a wide range of ability and attainment being taught or working together. Some of our long-standing beliefs about the need to separate the academically weak from the average, and their need for a reduced curriculum, are perhaps based on a reading and writing approach to teaching and learning which is no longer so pronounced.

17

Need for presentation of concepts through concrete experiences and examples

It is a well-established principle that the learning of slower children needs to be based on the concrete rather than abstractions. This is also true of average children but they are better able to move from concrete experiences to generalizing principles and the comprehension of abstract concepts. A common feature of the projects is that they recognize this need. There are undoubtedly ideas in the projects surveyed which, for their full comprehension, demand levels of abstract reasoning and judgement not attained by all disadvantaged children. But for the most part, the curriculum content of project materials is such that all except the most educationally retarded should be able to handle many of the ideas at the concrete level. It is, of course, very satisfying to a teacher when able children can develop from, say, experiences in the local environment a hypothesis which has general application. But it is of equal educational value if a less able group enthusiastically 'discovers' for itself something as apparently trivial as the fact that a park is used more during the evening than the day. For them, it is a step forward in awareness and in seeing relationships.

What is important is not so much the difficulty of the concepts as the teacher's awareness that disadvantaged children will have different levels of understanding. Some will have a mature understanding of processes and events which is in marked contrast to their inadequacies in literacy skills. Others may show only a poor understanding of the significance of experiments, visits and observations. If they are getting something from the experience appropriate to their stage of mental and educational development *as a step to further learning* the experiences have been worth while.

In brief, the question should not be 'Is this idea too difficult for these children to comprehend?' but 'Is it one which children of different levels of maturity can respond to in their own way and from which they can learn?'

The element of discussion and oral work

Discussion or verbal expression about observation and experience is an important element in all the projects considered. This facilitates recognition of the different levels of response referred to in the last paragraph. Oral work reduces some of the pressure on literacy skills as well as contributing to the improvement of oral language skills which is acknowledged to be a major objective in the education of the disadvantaged. It is hard for a teacher at any level to accept wholeheartedly that an idea expressed orally is as good as the same idea written down on paper. With many disadvantaged pupils we *must* accept this even

18

if we hope, as we should, that many will progress to adequate written expression.

Several of the projects surveyed offer considerable help to the teacher who has accepted that the improvement of language skills is one of his aims, but is uncertain how to put this into practice. The discussion approach of the Moral Education Project was successfully used even with educationally subnormal children; even the Humanities Curriculum Project approach was found effective with some groups of disadvantaged children. Projects in science, geography and mathematics offer ample scope for talk and discussion. In addition, there are the projects specifically concerned with the development of language skills.

Demands on reading and writing attainments should not prevent the participation of disadvantaged children

Teaching materials which require a reading ability of 11 years will automatically prevent a proportion (sometimes a very sizeable proportion) of pupils from benefiting – indeed, from participating. Much is said about the dangers of separating pupils in 'remedial' streams or special classes, but the dangers of pupils feeling set apart because they cannot follow the work, cannot write down what they know, require just as much emphasis.

One of the features of most of the projects studied (a feature not unique to Schools Council projects but well exemplified in them) is that the illiterate or semi-literate pupil can participate either without using reading and writing (Moral Education Project (13–16), the Social Education Project, Design and Craft); or with modified requirements for reading and writing (e.g. projects in science, mathematics and geography). This question is discussed in more detail on page 21.

The motivation appeal of curricula

The pupils we are concerned with are almost by definition those who are not motivated to achieve academic goals. Effort must be sustained by work which is related to their interests and experience or which is seen to have some relevance to what they do out of school, or what they are going to do after they leave school. There are, of course, older pupils (not only among the disadvantaged) who have virtually written school off and are resistant to any involvement.

Project materials have many characteristics which help in pupil motivation:

i Content which includes topics related to pupils' own experience and out-of-school interests (e.g. the topics raised in the Moral Education Project; studies of the local environment in relation to such topics as leisure facilities in the geography project; many of the topics in science projects which are relevant to world events – space, technology).

ii The emphasis on pupils' own activity, experiment and observation (e.g. Design and Craft, the science projects, Mathematics for the Majority, Language in Use).

iii Activities which are seen to be adult rather than childish – simple treatment of topics such as computers, probability, discussing adult issues such as relationships between the sexes, service in the community, large-scale projects in design and craft.

iv Work which enables the less able to work in partnership with more able children in projects, local studies, experiments and discussion.

v The possibility of a degree of successful achievement which does not depend on literacy.

vi Modes of teaching which involve pupils as partners in the learning process rather than as pupils to be instructed (e.g. projects which involve pupils in their own inquiries, which through discussion draw upon the pupils' own knowledge, experience and attitudes, or which, as in some of the mathematics and science work, require pupils to undertake experiments and to draw conclusions).

The integration of subject-matter

A continuing theme in discussion and writings about academically less successful pupils is the need to integrate subject-matter rather than to emphasize different subject disciplines. This is not to deny that some specialist teachers of history or geography are remarkably effective in presenting their subject to slow learners. But, in general, these pupils respond to broad themes which they can relate to their personal experience or which make them more aware of their experience. The particular knowledge and skills of specialists can be well used – even stretched – in this approach. A significant factor is that these pupils do not take easily to a timetable based on specialization and they take longer to adjust to the many different teachers involved.

Apart from those projects which set out to integrate studies, it is interesting to notice the many common themes and topics in different projects.

Factors affecting the use of projects with disadvantaged children

No one will pretend that the introduction of new curricula and methods is an easy undertaking, least of all with disadvantaged children. Many factors affect the successful adoption and use of project materials, some arising from the nature of the materials themselves.

The reading demands of project materials

Remedial teaching of reading has received a fair amount of attention and there is a useful range of reading laboratories, programmes for phonics teaching and easy reading books for older pupils. There has been less systematic consideration of procedures which would help poor readers to participate in general curriculum work – to the benefit not only of their general educational development but as a means of consolidating and extending such reading skills as they have acquired. The predicament of the very poor reader whose intelligence is average or above and who is interested in science or geography but continually frustrated by his poor reading particularly invites sympathetic concern.

As noted earlier, not all project materials demand good reading levels. The Moral Education Project (13–16) materials can be used with non-readers. Each unit of the *Man, Land and Leisure* theme in Geography for the Young School Leaver contains a wide range of resources – discussion sheets, slides, newspaper extracts, photo sheets, maps, statistics. It would be a simple matter to communicate to poor readers the gist of the popular newspaper articles used, but in any case the range and variety of materials is less forbidding than a textbook. Though the reading level required by the collections of evidence in the Humanities Curriculum Project packs is high, some teachers reported successful use with poor readers by careful selection of items, by using pictorial items, tapes or newspaper and magazine articles collected by pupils themselves. In science and mathematics projects much depends on the workcards and worksheets prepared by teachers. Examples of the preparation of simple worksheets are discussed in Chapter VII. Remedial teachers should be in a position to offer practical help to specialist colleagues over readability and presentation.

The selection or preparation of suitable material is, of course, an added burden for a teacher who may already have enough to cope with in organizing experiments and getting to grips with the aims and methods of the project. It would be an advantage if future development projects were asked to consider the inclusion of a teacher of slow learners in the project team or on the consultative committee. He could assist teams in writing materials in such a way that the range of pupils who could use them was widened. This is not too difficult, nor does it necessarily

21

mean 'writing down' – often clear, direct exposition is something that would benefit all pupils. The remedial teacher, especially if he has some acquaintance with studies of children's vocabulary and language, is often able to point out places where a change of word or phrase or simplification of a sentence pattern would help the poorer reader without any loss of meaning. Such a team member could also be concerned with the provision of additional pictorial and taped materials, since remedial teachers have considerable experience in the preparation and use of such materials for poor readers. It would be an advantage if project teams could produce simplified sample worksheets.

There is, of course, a limit to the simplification which is possible. It is worth noting, therefore, that we received evidence that some pupils with fairly low reading ages were managing to extract the sense of passages which might have been thought too difficult – for example, in science. Many things, of course, affect the difficulty of the reading. The type-face, size and layout can deter or attract the poor reader. Readability depends not only on the words, the length of sentence and the style but also on the context in which reading takes place. If the topic is one which pupils know something about and are interested in, or if the reading occurs in the context of some experiment or activity, the difficulty of the passage or worksheet may be reduced. For example, a poor reader is sometimes able to puzzle out the instructions for something he is keen to do, aided by a diagram and spurred on by his desire to see the end-product.

Many of the poor readers we are concerned with have sufficient ability to make an attempt at the required reading, but they read slowly and are held up by unfamiliar words. They are therefore impeded in comprehension and, above all, find reading a tiring and distasteful process. Awareness of this and some help with unfamiliar words could ease the problem. In classes where there are a number of poor readers, it would help to discuss and draw attention to unfamiliar words or technical terms before reading a passage. Even if difficulties remained (and the difficulty might well be confusion over small common words), it would be a benefit for pupils to feel that their problem was recognized and accepted, and that they were being given some assistance. A readiness to ask the teacher or another pupil for help in reading an unknown word should also be encouraged. Unfortunately, some poor readers fear ridicule or condemnation and try by all sorts of means to conceal the full extent of their reading inadequacy. (Sometimes this shows as apparent apathy or lack of interest.) Ideally, their reading failure should be seen by themselves and by others not as failure but as a disability which, like a visual defect, must be circumvented as far as possible. A number of the reports we received mentioned the help given to poor readers by better ones, or the paraphrasing of information which some pupils would not be able to read.

Another line of approach to this problem concerns the role of remedial teachers.

Although the teaching of reading to the poorest readers in school is more than sufficient to occupy their time, their knowledge and experience would be well used if they acted as resource teachers, advising others on the preparation of suitable materials and the use of audio-visual aids. In team-teaching situations a remedial teacher would be a valuable member of the team in relation to children with the poorest literacy skills – for example, giving special attention to reading unavoidable technical terms.

The problem is that there are not enough remedial teachers, and the kind of help we are discussing must depend in most cases on the specialist teacher's awareness of the problems. This is yet another argument for all teachers to have some acquaintance, in initial and in-service training, with the problems of the poor reader. Our own experience is that teachers in training are much more interested in these problems than they were a few years ago. We would recommend that, in addition to lectures and reading, there should be opportunity for teachers in training to have some practical study in this field – not necessarily actual remedial teaching of reading (though this, of course, would be valuable), but the examination of books, workbooks and other materials for remedial reading. A readability formula* can be used to compare the difficulty of several passages and books – and this can be taken a step further to include the rewriting of difficult material in an easier form. Even a little time given to these problems in initial training would be sufficient to evoke some interest in and awareness of them. There are few teachers of specialist subjects who will not encounter these problems.

Reducing the demands for written work

Even when remedial reading has resulted in the achievement of a useful degree of reading ability, spelling and the ability to express ideas in writing often remain very poor and any quantity of written work, unless the pupil is very highly motivated, is a distasteful activity. As suggested earlier, an oral response is often not valued as much as a written one – or if it is, teachers may still feel that they ought to have something more tangible to show for their efforts. Yet it is not a lowering of standards to accept an oral explanation or an adequate discussion as a satisfactory outcome of learning. In fact, it is the first priority and written expression the second.

It is to be hoped that small portable cassette recorders will be more widely accepted as *essential* equipment for use with less successful pupils, both for providing information and for recording pupils' responses.

It is, of course, beneficial for children to attempt a written response as well. This will often mean assessing the idea being expressed and being tolerant of the

* See J. Gilliland, *Readability* (University of London Press, 1972).

23

spelling, style and handwriting used. On page 128 there are examples of written work in mathematics by a child very handicapped in spelling and expression. If correctness had been insisted on, it is unlikely that her interest in the topics studied would have persisted. Incidentally, in such a case the remedial teacher can use the words mis-spelt to build up spelling lists of more frequently used words. It is important to give such pupils a technique for learning to spell words and these lists could be the basis for weekly assignments in spelling. Bad spellers sometimes have continued difficulty with the common, often short, words but if they are given a technique for scrutinizing and learning words, they are more competent with technical words newly met in various school subjects. The practice of drawing attention to new words being introduced in a topic or lesson, partly to ensure knowledge of their meaning and partly to assist with spelling, is a help to the disadvantaged.

Several schools we observed were making good use of worksheets prepared to suit poorer readers and requiring the minimum of writing – one word or a short phrase for responses.

Many 'slow learners' ought to be given systematic help with handwriting to correct inefficient ways of forming letters and joins.* Help of this kind improves their work and morale.

Modification of examinations

Little information was received about the modification of examinations apart from one case in which the language laboratory was used to give 'remedial' children orally the same test which others in the age group had been given as a written test (see page 121). The requirement in some schools that all pupils should take the same written examination is often a matter of considerable concern to remedial teachers and has a demoralizing effect on pupils who have a reasonable knowledge of a subject but are unable to read and write well enough to sit a written examination. It would seem that where other forms of assessment are not considered sufficient, a modified examination or an oral examination like the one described earlier is desirable. In this connexion, Schools Council Examinations Bulletin 21, *CSE: an Experiment in the Oral Examining of Chemistry*,† has some pertinent observations to make about devising an oral examination. Apart from advice on the conduct of the examination (e.g. the question of prompting), it points out the healthy 'backwash' effect, in that discussion which would become a necessary part of preparation work could promote the effective use of spoken English.

* See A. Inglis and E. Connel, *The Teaching of Handwriting* (Nelson, 1964).
† Evans/Methuen Educational, 1971.

Difficulties in introducing pupils to new approaches

New approaches often require considerable readjustment on the part of the teacher. They also make new demands on pupils, and it is not surprising that children often need time to adjust to new ways. For example, we heard of pupils gathered together for discussion who remained virtually silent. How well pupils will respond to the opportunity for discussion depends, among other things, on what experience they have had of talk and discussion in their previous schooling. In this connexion several schools claimed that the disadvantaged talked freely, whereas the more able ones were inhibited. The remedial pupils are often more accustomed to a free interchange of talk with a remedial teacher, and are perhaps less worried about giving the 'right' answer.

Similarly, the readiness to engage in role-play or dramatization is likely to depend on previous experience and we were impressed with the gradual preparation for and initiation into this kind of activity undertaken by the Social Education project at Nottingham. (See page 60.)

The teachers' guide to the *Man, Land and Leisure* theme in Geography for the Young School Leaver materials included a statement which can be applied over the entire range of projects we have looked at: *'the whole pattern of approach in devising the learning experience with its emphasis on pupil involvement is likely to be most successful where a similar emphasis is being developed with the younger age groups in school.'* While this is true for all children, it is likely to be particularly important for less successful pupils. They are more likely to be hampered by diffidence and lack of confidence arising from educational failure or emotional difficulties, or by their weakness in communication. It should be said, however, that in the information we received from schools and projects there are numerous examples of disadvantaged children responding well to methods requiring activity, inquiry and discussion. Freed from the constraints of their literacy problems, they are often able to perform nearer to the level of their age group.

It is also true that the ability to work in groups is something that grows with practice. Some younger or less mature or very slow children are scarcely ready for working together and need a more gradual introduction to co-operation. A difficult problem is that of the less able child being given a too undemanding task in a group activity or being carried as a passenger. There is no clear-cut solution to this except to consider carefully the composition of groups and to try to ensure that each child has the opportunity to make some genuine contribution.

The problem of maintaining interest and motivation

Schools referred frequently to the need to select topics from courses, either because there was too much ground to cover in a complete course, or in order to avoid difficult concepts, or to offer material of interest to particular groups. Teachers have sometimes been surprised at the degree of interest shown in concepts that they would have thought too difficult. It is probably fair to suggest that what matters is not only the difficulty of concepts but also whether they excite interest and curiosity; not only the relevance to the pupil's own experience but also whether they provoke a new kind of experience or enjoyment. The dangers of relying too much on novelty are well known, but novelty can be a starting point for the disadvantaged. It is often necessary to plan short projects and use topics which show results quickly, rather than to attempt an extended sequence of learning. As one school put it, 'long-term objectives mean little – so short-term objectives are posed so that success is reinforced.'

The importance of facilitating success and of immediate rather than delayed satisfaction is a basic principle in teaching less successful pupils which could well be overlooked by specialist teachers accustomed to taking a longer view of a course of learning.

It often happens that what interests disadvantaged children is not strictly relevant to the learning in hand. Some experience incidental to the main inquiry may spark off enthusiasm. It is often worth following up such an interest or capitalizing on incidental experiences which may produce a higher level of involvement.

Factors in the school affecting the use of project materials with disadvantaged children

The first and most important factor is the school's attitude towards the least successful pupils and its views about what they can be expected to achieve. While it is necessary to be aware of their difficulties and limitations, it is also important not to expect too little; with suitable preparation and careful presentation these pupils often do better than expected. Implicit in many replies we received from schools was a desire to identify and provide for the needs of disadvantaged pupils. On visits and at conferences we found many indications of concern for the problems of slower children. Yet few would deny that less progress has been achieved in this area than in many others as *Slow Learners in Secondary Schools** shows clearly. One can speculate on the reasons for this: the priority given to courses leading to tangible academic results; the tendency for responsibility for planning courses or organization to be in the hands of those whose experience has been with average or above-average pupils; the severe shortage of teachers with

* Department of Education and Science, Education Survey 15 (H M S O, 1971).

experience, training and, above all, the ability and personality for responsible posts in connexion with slow-learning pupils.

The basic problem is to recognize and provide for the less successful pupils' different needs, and yet not to limit their educational opportunities and experiences. Until fairly recently it was almost universally accepted that these pupils were best catered for in streamed classes where the work could be adapted to their needs. In the last few years, there has been some movement away from the practice of streaming, though *Slow Learners in Secondary Schools* reporting a survey in 1967–68 found a majority of schools (104 out of 158) organizing their pupils in streams according to ability – twenty-four schools had broad-banded parallel streams, and thirty-six schools had intermediate arrangements such as unstreamed classes for the younger pupils and streamed for the older.

The complex issue of school organization in relation to the least successful pupils cannot be summed up in a simple judgement for or against streaming. There are many factors to consider in practice: there are various ways of organizing by setting; schools vary in the proportion of able and less able pupils and in other characteristics of their intake; schools also vary in the nature of their buildings, resources and staff. There are, however, a number of considerations which point to the desirability of avoiding rigid classification of less successful pupils, especially if such classification prevents them from experiencing a wide range of curriculum opportunities:

1 Less successful pupils are a varied group. Though they have below-average attainments, it does not follow that they are limited in ability or that their levels of ability and attainment will necessarily remain low. With remedial help and the stimulation of a wider curriculum, both ability and attainment may improve.
2 Unsuccessful pupils are not necessarily weak in every subject. Many are relatively more competent in some areas than others and capable of working with interest and success in some subjects with more able pupils.
3 Separating less successful pupils into lower streams carries the danger of reinforcing feelings of failure, perpetuating their own lower aspirations and teachers' lower expectations.

As suggested earlier, the emphasis in projects on discussion, inquiry and activity has to some extent narrowed the gap between the teaching of average and below-average pupils even though eventual achievements will be different. In the case of certain projects, there would be no inherent difficulty in using the teaching materials with groups of mixed ability, and in others such as science projects,

27

in which some adjustment is required for slow learners, we were impressed by reports and observations of classes of mixed ability.

It is important, of course, that the widening of opportunities and experience does not weaken the provision for special needs and requirements. Apart from the continuing need of some pupils for remedial teaching, disadvantaged pupils (especially the truly slow learners, and the younger age groups) need someone who provides a secure relationship and takes a personal interest. Almost certainly what matters most are the attitudes of the school towards the less successful – attitudes which are communicated in many aspects of the life and work of the school. One of the chief ways in which a positive attitude towards disadvantaged children can be communicated is by modifying the course content and methods of teaching so that these children are able to participate as fully as possible in a range of curricular activities.

Difficulties for the teacher

Although a teacher might agree that a particular project's materials have something to offer in the teaching of disadvantaged children, there are many factors affecting its successful adoption and use. In general, most projects imply a form of teaching which involves more activity by the class. This can require considerable organization in the preparation of materials, worksheets and the deployment of other resources such as audio-visual aids. The course to be followed may be less formally laid down than has usually been the case with academic courses leading to examinations; what develops depends on pupil participation and initiative or on the course of discussion.

The teacher will need to assimilate information from a teacher's guide (perhaps several) and to acquire a thorough knowledge of the materials which in the case of some projects is a considerable undertaking.

For some teachers all this amounts to a readjustment in their style of teaching. Trying to cater for the needs of disadvantaged children requires further readjustments – not only the adaptation of materials and teaching methods, but also readjusting expectations of what can be achieved and evaluation of the benefits accruing.

It is obviously important, therefore, for teachers to be adequately prepared in the use of project materials. It was our impression that teachers using the Humanities Curriculum Project materials who were fully conversant with the aims, procedures and their justification tended to be more successful. In science and mathematics projects, schools which had been closely involved with the project team, or where one experienced member of staff was able to advise and guide his colleagues, were, not surprisingly, more likely to report successful experience.

28

It is also important that teachers working with disadvantaged children should have more opportunities for discussing the particular problems of using project materials with these children. We include among our recommendations, therefore, several steps which could be taken through in-service training to facilitate discussion of issues raised in this report.

III. Recommendations and implications for future development

This chapter makes a number of recommendations arising from our survey and also discusses some issues relevant to the future development of work with disadvantaged children.

Dissemination of information about the use of project materials with disadvantaged children

We have concluded that a number of projects are immediately appropriate for teaching disadvantaged children and that others can be used with some selection and adaptation. Nevertheless, the indications from our survey are that Schools Council and other projects are not very well known by remedial teachers and that there may even be a tendency to assume that they are not relevant to the education of slower children. Our recommendations follow.

1 *Project teams and organizations concerned with in-service training should be encouraged to arrange courses on the use of project materials with slow-learning and disadvantaged children.*

Such courses would promote awareness of the potential of appropriate projects for enriching the education of disadvantaged children, and increase awareness in project teams and in teachers of specialist subjects of the particular needs of the disadvantaged. It was our experience that project teams were interested in this problem and able to refer to examples of work being done. A session on slow learners within a general course is valuable, but the topic is of sufficient importance to merit courses and conferences devoted entirely to the use of projects with disadvantaged children. It is important, of course, that such courses should be not only for remedial teachers but also for teachers of specialist subjects and others with responsibility in schools.

2 *Teachers' centres should initiate groups of specialist and remedial teachers for examining project materials in relation to the curricular needs of slow-learning and disadvantaged children.*

We wrote during the year to 420 teachers' centres. We had thirty-four replies, of which eighteen gave information about groups of teachers meeting to discuss curricula for slow learners. Several centre wardens said they felt there was a need for more activity in this area!

3 *One-year courses of further study, whether in special and remedial education or in particular subject areas, should include an examination of Schools Council and other projects in relation to disadvantaged children.*

During the year, we wrote to tutors of one-year courses in special and remedial education and the small response suggests lack of awareness of the projects available. A study of projects in such courses would provide an effective and practical way of covering a number of curricular issues.

4 *Schools with a high proportion of disadvantaged children should receive financial assistance over and above the normal capitation in order to buy the materials and equipment needed to make use of recent work in curriculum development.*

Despite the obvious relevance of much of the material, relatively few schools seemed to be much influenced by Schools Council and other projects unless they had been directly involved at the trial stage. The cost of published materials was mentioned, and this may be a factor in ordering materials which might not be found suitable or adaptable for the special needs of less able children. It was suggested that, as part of a process of positive discrimination, schools with a large proportion of disadvantaged children should have the opportunity to experiment with project materials. Some LEAs do help over this by purchasing project materials and organizing courses for teachers on their use. This has happened with *Breakthrough to Literacy* and also with science and mathematics project materials which are often disseminated through mathematics and science centres. Where such a policy is not practised, schools which could clearly benefit from project materials are often unable to buy them. It is clear that schools with a large proportion of disadvantaged children need specially generous provision for teaching resources.

Curriculum development

It is apparent that whether curriculum materials are used, and used successfully, with disadvantaged children depends upon the sympathetic interest, the experience and skill of teachers as well as the expenditure of extra time and effort required to organize and prepare additional teaching materials. We consider that more could be done to assist teachers using materials over the whole range of ability. Our recommendations follow.

5 *Consideration should be given in the future to the inclusion in certain project teams of a teacher experienced with disadvantaged or slow-learning children.*

This could be justified on the grounds that up to twenty per cent of pupils are likely to have some difficulty with materials because of their language, reading and conceptual demands. A teacher experienced with these difficulties could give advice within the team about content and presentation, and could be especially involved in trials of the materials with less successful pupils. The teachers' guides of several projects have included a short section on the needs of slow learners. The inclusion of a remedial teacher in a project team would surely lead to a much more thorough discussion of practical problems and of examples of good practice.

The matters with which he would be concerned are not, of course, relevant only to the teaching of less successful pupils. As schools move away from streamed to mixed-ability groupings, teachers are brought face to face with a reality that homogeneous grouping tends to hide: that individuals and groups vary widely in their abilities and in the experiences they bring to the learning situation. Many of the generalizations made in Chapter II are equally applicable to average children – even if they are less crucial.

6 *A development project should be set up, the aim of which would be the preparation of materials in conjunction with certain existing projects, for use with slow-learning and disadvantaged children.*

We have concluded that some project materials (such as those from the Moral Education (13–16) and the Science 5–13 projects) can be used without too much difficulty with disadvantaged children. Certain other projects (such as the Humanities Curriculum Project, Integrated Studies and Religious Education) offer valuable approaches and materials but different materials could be prepared better suited to these pupils. The kinds of materials we have in mind include the following:

a   Simple workcards and worksheets which could be duplicated for use in courses for slow learners and also act as models of what is required.

b   Additional pictorial or taped material to supplement or act as an alternative to existing written material.

32

c   Notes and guidance about the use of these and other materials and particularly about the use of audio-visual resources.

d   Materials, information and reference books with an easy reading vocabulary yet with an appearance and format acceptable to older pupils. In the science, social studies and humanities areas, there is a gap which has been long recognized yet never filled, partly because there was no framework of curriculum practice within which to start writing.

The main point is that the poor reader should have available material suited to his reading level in those fields where curriculum activities have aroused his interest. He should not always have to fall back on adventures and teenage stories for reading matter.

It would be an advantage for such a development project to work closely with the experienced teams of particular curriculum projects so that the preparation of additional materials for slow learners was in harmony with the aims and approach of projects. The Humanities Curriculum Project is one example. There would be no problem in producing collections of evidence which, as well as providing easier reading material, made greater use of pictorial and taped material. The approach of the Integrated Studies Project is a potentially valuable one for disadvantaged children and it would be particularly useful if a development project prepared some material suited to slower children. Similarly, the Religious Education in Secondary Schools Project has produced a wealth of ideas, some of which could be adapted for slow learners.

7 *Alternatively, it might be best to concentrate on a curriculum development project in humanities for slow-learning and disadvantaged children.*

Our survey indicates that the science projects referred to in Chapter VII and the Mathematics for the Majority Continuation Project are capable of relatively easy adaptation for use with less successful pupils. Although we had some interesting reports of work in humanities (Chapter V), the need for modified materials is most apparent in this area. A project of this kind would obviously draw upon the experience and approaches of existing projects in humanities but could take a fresh look at the problem. As suggested on page 86, there is a pressing need to develop this area of education for these pupils. Their own experience often relates closely to the topics considered in parts of humanities courses, but they have often had too little opportunity to think about and discuss the issues in a systematic way. Yet these courses can be the hardest to teach satisfactorily to children who have difficulty with the concepts and with communication, as well as literacy skills.

Educating pupils with limited literacy skills

We should like at this point to focus attention on the need to examine methods and techniques of educating pupils with limited reading and writing skills and the need to disseminate knowledge about such methods.

In the post-war period, especially since the first surveys of backwardness in reading, we have been aware of pupils whose poor reading and writing impeded their academic progress. The extent of this problem can be gauged by the findings of the Department of Education and Science Education Survey 15, *Slow Learners in Secondary Schools*,* which stated on the basis of headteachers' estimates that fourteen per cent of secondary pupils needed special educational help. Even when remedial reading is effective in improving the reading levels of these pupils, we know that reading often continues to be an unrewarding activity for them and moreover that spelling and written work may remain weak.

While we have for a long time been aware of pupils of average intelligence with severe reading difficulties, more recent public and professional interest in these difficulties (often focused by the use of the term dyslexia) has stimulated concern and the feeling that more should be done. While remedial teaching enables some to recover from their disability, others not getting sufficiently specialized help drag out their schooldays, rarely experiencing the enjoyment of success in learning things of which they are intellectually capable. The experience of LEA classes and schemes run by voluntary organizations for teaching adult non-readers is further evidence that this is a significant problem.

The trend towards mixed-ability grouping and providing curricula for use over the whole ability range also increases the need to examine more thoroughly the ways in which less successful pupils can be enabled to participate in and benefit from wider curriculum experiences.

In brief, there is a sizeable proportion of the secondary-school population with a significant weakness in literacy skills. Yet in an era of television and audio-visual resources, their educational development is still too often impeded by the barrier of the written word. Our recommendations follow.

---

8 *Measures should be taken to examine ways in which semi-literate pupils can continue to learn in spite of their disability.*

The development project we have proposed would of course have to examine this question in relation to the preparation of teaching materials and the use of a variety of resources. But systematic studies could be undertaken in other ways – for example, by organizations and teacher education institutions concerned with

* HMSO, 1971.

educational technology and educational television. There appear to be only a few reports of research or surveys of practice in this area.

9 *One or more centres should be established which could focus attention on materials and techniques for use with these pupils and which could act as a source of advice and a means of disseminating information.*

A resources centre based, perhaps, at a college of education could maintain a close watch on equipment developments and could explore the use of equipment in remedial departments, remedial services and special schools, as well as encourage and take part in the development of teaching materials in the main curriculum areas to assist teachers of disadvantaged children.

Changing role of remedial departments in secondary schools

Changes in organization within secondary schools have already resulted in changes in the functions of remedial departments and in the methods of working of remedial teachers. The challenge to remedial teachers to assist in the widening of curricular opportunities for disadvantaged children is a further factor in this process of change.

Our small-scale survey provides too little information on which to make judgements about this important topic but no doubt the Schools Council Project on the Curricular Needs of Slow Learning Pupils (1971–74) will be able to assess the current position and discuss possible developments.

However, it is clear that remedial teachers and teachers of specialist subjects should work more closely together in the planning of curricula for disadvantaged children, in the preparation of materials and the organization of teaching. Traditional concepts of the role and expertise of both the remedial teacher and teacher of specialist subjects are changing. The remedial teacher is not just someone who can teach backward readers or who is 'good with backward children', the one who can take care of the difficult cases. His role should increasingly include advisory functions in relation to the teaching of less successful pupils, and he should be, where possible, a member of teaching teams, giving advice about grouping, materials and techniques which will assist the process of opening up curriculum opportunities to disadvantaged children. He might base more of his remedial teaching upon the reading, spelling and writing needs encountered by remedial pupils in general curriculum areas and see one aspect of remedial work as helping children to consolidate, extend and use their literacy skills in science, humanities and other fields.

It is equally apparent that the teacher of specialist subjects has to develop an understanding of the difficulties and needs of less successful pupils and how teaching has to be modified and organized for groups of wide ranges of ability. Teaching children in the lower ranges of ability and attainment is not a mystery known only to remedial teachers. The basis of it is good teaching which starts from where pupils are in their understanding, experience and motivation and which assesses how far and by what means further progress can be made through the organization of learning experiences. Every good teacher from nursery to university level has to do this. The difference is that good teaching of this kind is crucial for slow-learning and disadvantaged pupils who have few resources for helping themselves if the teaching is not appropriate. The special experience of the remedial teacher can help here.

This widening of teaching expertise and co-operation between the work of remedial and specialist subject teachers is essential in opening up curriculum opportunities for disadvantaged children. At the same time, we are very conscious of the fact that where necessary modifications of teaching and material have not been made, the backward child in a non-streamed situation can feel even more isolated by his incapacity than in a remedial class. We are also conscious of the pronounced need of some of the least successful pupils for someone in school who provides a secure base or a psychological anchor and we would not want this function of the remedial teacher to be lost – unless it were provided in other ways.

The initial and in-service training of teachers

Much of this report has important implications for the initial and further training of teachers. There are four main recommendations.

10 *Teachers of specialist subjects will increasingly be teaching groups with a wide range of ability. Their initial training, therefore, should acquaint them with the needs of less successful pupils and how these can be catered for in terms of content of courses and modifications of teaching method and organization.*

The emphasis should be on the practical steps that can be taken. Once interest is aroused there are plenty of sources of further reading about the difficulties and needs of disadvantaged children.

To judge from our experiences in conducting this survey, those involved in training and advising teachers are concerned about this problem and are ready to look more closely at what is required – although they are often diffident about their lack of special knowledge in this field. As we suggest elsewhere, the special expertise can be over-emphasized. What is needed at the training level, as at the school level, is co-operation between the remedial specialist and the tutors for specialist subjects.

11 *The training and recruitment of teachers for remedial posts in secondary schools should be studied as a matter of urgency.*

It is clear that the expertise of the remedial teacher in a secondary school includes more than the ability to teach basic educational skills and more than the ability to establish positive relationships with less successful pupils. He needs to have sufficient insight into the work of other specialist teachers to be able to discuss their work with slower children, to be able to advise on the use of appropriate media and resources, and generally to work in a team with other specialists. There is unfortunately a shortage of teachers with the interest, experience and ability for these posts. One factor relevant to this shortage is the mode of recruitment. This is largely left to chance. We know where the future science or mathematics specialists are coming from, but we have no organized way of ensuring that young teachers in colleges of education and university departments of education are given the opportunity to become aware of remedial work as an important and valuable aspect of teaching. For those who do become interested, there are too few opportunities for further training.

12 *This initial preparation should be followed up by more attention during in-service training to the teaching of slow learners in general curriculum areas.*

As suggested earlier, courses and working groups in teachers' centres should be attracting not only the staff of remedial departments but the heads and members of other departments whose teaching inevitably includes the less successful twenty per cent of the population.

13 *Consideration might be given to establishing centres to provide a consultancy service for schools and in-service training.*

The use of a wider range of curriculum resources and the need for a wider dissemination of knowledge about methods of teaching the disadvantaged calls for a greater availability of advice on materials, resources and teaching methods. These centres might be based on the specialist advisory service of an LEA, on teachers' centres, on an area resources centre or on a region. The staff should certainly include remedial teachers of proven success, seconded on either a part-time or full-time basis. The existence of such centres would give identity to a particular kind of expertise required in meeting the educational needs of the least successful twenty per cent of the secondary-school population, and could facilitate its development.

Part 2

Survey of the use of project materials with disadvantaged children

IV. English

This chapter reviews projects concerned with teaching English, both as the mother tongue and as a second language.

The brief of the Nuffield Programme in Linguistics and English Teaching (1964–67), directed by Professor M. A. K. Halliday, was to look at developments in linguistics and their relevance to the teaching of English. When the programme was taken over by the Schools Council (1967–71), the work was carried forward as two linked projects associated within one programme but with different objectives. One, the Initial Literacy Project, was concerned with the initial teaching of reading and writing; its work has been published as *Breakthrough to Literacy*. The other, the Language in Use Project, was concerned with older secondary pupils, but in the course of development the materials proved suitable for use throughout the secondary school. Both projects were based at University College London.

Breakthrough to Literacy

These materials, developed by David Mackay (project organizer), Brian Thompson and Pamela Schaub, and published by Longman, provide an approach to the initial teaching of reading and writing. Although primarily intended for young children beginning reading, the scheme has also been used by remedial teachers at the primary school stage, by special school teachers and by some remedial teachers at the secondary stage.

One of the fundamental beliefs of the project is that reading matter should from the beginning of reading be linked to the child's own language. The child begins, therefore, by composing and reading his own short sentences which express his own experience. He does this using a 'sentence maker', consisting of a folder with pockets, in which are stored a set of cards with words, word-endings and punctuation printed on them, making up a collection of 130 items. These items are built round words found to be commonly used by young children in this activity. There are also blank cards on which other words relevant to the child may be written. A plastic stand is provided into which the cards can be slotted to form sentences.

The advantage of this kind of approach to reading is that the child is initially composing and reading back his own sentences using his own vocabulary. It avoids the stilted and unnatural sentences of some beginning reading books and enables the child to compose and read something related to his personal experience. It is in line with a common remedial practice of getting a child to make up his own topic or reading book, but at the beginning it removes the difficulty of writing. There are some incidental benefits in that the child practises recognition and discrimination in finding the word he wants, and in replacing it in the folder he has to match it against the word printed in the appropriate place in the folder.

It will be apparent that for non-readers or very poor readers at the secondary stage this could be a new and motivating approach. The 130 printed items provided were selected on the basis of experience with infant children, but the blank cards can be used to write out the words which the older child needs.

The Sentence Maker is provided in two forms – a large version to be used by the teacher of a group of children, and smaller ones for each child. Other material includes a magnet board and figurines for assisting with the essential language work, nursery rhymes on cards, a record, and short reading books, but since these have been prepared with young children in mind, they are not likely to be used with older children.

However, the Word Maker (now called First Word Maker) used to introduce phonics would be useful with older children. This is a folder with pockets containing printed symbols (such as *sh, o, p*, for making *shop*) and with this the child can experiment in constructing words and can learn how words are made. The approach is linguistically sound and since remedial teachers of older children sometimes need guidance about the teaching of phonics, the Word Maker and the advice given in the excellent Teacher's Manual are strongly recommended. The manual is not only a guide to the use of the materials but is also a short and readable statement of a linguistic approach to teaching reading. It includes useful advice on spelling, handwriting and written English and also some accounts of *Breakthrough* in use in secondary and special schools.

Breakthrough to Literacy was in use in a wide variety of schools all over Britain at the time of our survey in the autumn term of 1971. Questionnaires revealed that it was in use in a variety of special schools and in a number of secondary schools. The materials had considerable flexibility in use and produced favourable reactions from teachers of children with learning difficulties of all kinds.

A South Wales junior school

Used within a remedial reading unit. The unit has 130 retarded readers – thirteen groups, usually of ten children. Groups have one- or two-hour sessions per week and children are withdrawn from classes. *Breakthrough* is introduced at 7 years old. Most of them are able to write without the aid of the Sentence Maker by age 9. About ten minutes of the one-hour session devoted to oral work. Used Sentence Maker with dyslexic child who has benefited.

A Midlands remedial department

Breakthrough appeared to use all the best principles in the teaching of reading and the manual was thought to be one of the most useful books on the teaching of reading yet produced.

A school for ESN children

Used with junior children who are enthusiastic. Used by most of a class of twenty 9- to 10-year-olds, and most of a class of twenty 10- to 11-year-olds. Much oral work done with Magnet Board and Teacher's Sentence Maker. Word Maker not attempted.

Remedial Education Service, Midlands

Used by peripatetic teachers teaching 7- to 13-year-olds. Used by withdrawal groups in junior schools. Most successful when used with groups of non-readers not exceeding eight. Initially oral work comprises 90 per cent of the reading session, reducing to about 50 per cent. Word Makers are not yet used.

Special education unit

Breakthrough is especially useful for children at the beginning of the reading process. When children have a reading age of $6\frac{1}{2}$ to 7 years the material becomes cumbersome and other methods are more effective. The Word Maker is not used. Little use is made of the spelling section, although I would agree that the manual is extremely good on this.

The head of a remedial department in a Welsh country secondary school wrote as follows:

The only Schools Council project material used by my department is *Breakthrough to Literacy*. This project is basically one for use in the infants and lower junior school. However some secondary schools were included in the pilot scheme. I accepted the opportunity to try out this project with some of the poorer readers in Year 1.

In Year 1 we have made use of the scheme and it seems to be successful. The words used in the child's Sentence Maker seem to be ideally suited for the child's environment and vocabulary. They are words which he uses in everyday communication, consequently the Sentence Maker gives the child a definite interest. Any additional words other than those in the Sentence Maker are written out by the children on printed inserts. This gives the child the feeling of doing everything himself. The teacher thus remains as an adviser. Some of the children in Year 1 with poor reading ages are started on *Breakthrough to Literacy*. When they are allowed to make up sentences of their own the children are obviously very enthusiastic. Having mastered the words in the Sentence Maker, the children then proceed with another reading scheme.

Not all teachers found the material congenial, and several commented on difficulties of organization. One school found that the materials were too fragmented: 'it was agreed that the idea was of value but we found that administration was difficult.' Some offered constructive suggestions for improvement or modification. A day special school found that the Teacher's Sentence Maker was more useful to them than the children's version because in the latter the printed words were too closely packed together. (The First Word Maker has been made larger.) For a similar reason, the children's Word Maker folders were not much used and the teacher thought it would be a good idea if symbols were on magnetized cards that would work on the magnet-board principle. This school had not made much use of the cut-out pictures as the teacher preferred to draw on the board to illustrate a topic. However, the little reading books appealed to all the children in the age range (up to 10+, IQs 50–75). The teacher concluded, 'On the whole I have found the *Breakthrough* scheme helpful and am sure that for children of average ability it is a very well thought out scheme covering most aspects of normal reading development. I think the scheme is good also for ESN children at a certain stage and I will continue to use it where appropriate.'

A teacher of the deaf had been using the material with children with impaired hearing. This teacher found that the *Breakthrough to Literacy* materials were useful because the children's own short, simple sentences about familiar situations experienced at school or home helped both their language and their reading. The children also liked the *Breakthrough* books which, because they were short and could be finished fairly quickly, gave them a sense of success. (Books in the Green Set, published in 1973, are specifically designed for older less-able children.)

At a London borough remedial reading centre, the materials had been used with small groups of 11- to 13-year-olds. The great majority of the pupils were Irish or West Indian, mostly slow learners, but the occasional pupil was above average 'with perceptual difficulties of one kind or another'. In the teacher's opinion, no two children seemed to have similar problems and it was for this reason that *Breakthrough to Literacy* had proved so useful. In January 1971, the reading ages of her pupils were between 5·2 and 5·9 years on the Schonell G W R test. By December, there had been improvement to 7·6 to 8·9 years. Initially the only reading material used was derived from *Breakthrough*. This teacher thought the great advantage was in the teaching of endings, particularly in such words as 'goes' and 'does', and she found it possible to use *Breakthrough* in combination with S R A word games. She had used *Breakthrough* to teach phonics but in her own way; she had found it useful to make cards with *ea, oa, ee, ou, ow, oi, oy* symbols on them. (The new Second Word Maker, published in 1973, also does this.)

Summary

The replies we have received about the use of *Breakthrough* in a variety of special and ordinary schools and remedial services indicate that the approach has been found useful with many kinds of pupils at the beginning stages of reading. The blank cards in the Sentence Maker mean that a reading vocabulary can be built up on the basis of the older child's interests and experiences, and the method overcomes the problem of finding sufficiently simple beginning reading material for the older non-reader which is not too young in content. The replies received do not indicate so much use of the Word Maker, perhaps because schools have other methods and materials in use. However, developing an awareness of the structure of words is frequently an important need for older backward readers; the guidance about phonics and spelling in the *Teacher's Manual* repays study.

Language in Use

This project offers a stimulating approach to English. Teaching materials were produced by Peter Doughty (Director of the project from January 1971), John Pearce and Geoffrey Thornton, and published in 1971 by Edward Arnold in loose-leaf form in a ring binder. The material is in three parts and each part is subdivided into themes:

Part 1 The nature and function of language
a   Using language to convey information
b   Using language expressively
c   Sound and symbol
d   Pattern in language.

Part 2 Language and individual man
a Language and reality
b Language and culture
c Language and experience.
Part 3 Language and social man
a Language in individual relationships
b Language in social relationships
c Language in social organizations.

A number of units for each theme are suggested in the notes. For example, the theme 'Language in social relationships' includes the following units:

Belonging to a group
How adults see teenagers
Crowds
Social talk
What is conversation?
Conversation between friends
Family talk
Being interviewed
Interviews on television
Talking on the telephone
Taking messages.

For each unit the notes suggest a number of activities which could be undertaken in several sessions. Teachers are free to select, adapt and extend the activities suggested.

For example, one of the units in the theme 'Using language to convey information' is 'New words' (A9). It considers how new terms arise because distinctions have to be made as a consequence of new discoveries. It suggests examination of the need to invent new words and the way in which such words can come to be regarded as jargon. There would be little difficulty in getting a remedial class to compile in a first session a list of new or 'special' words they have met – trendy, dishy, gear, satellite, astronaut – and to sort them out into technical terms and others. The notes suggest that in a second session consideration should be given to the origins, contexts and uses of some of these words, and that in a third session short pieces of writing for different purposes could be undertaken in groups, so that pupils become aware of the need for technical terms in different kinds of communication.

Although the unit refers to several contexts with which slow learners might not be familiar, it would not be difficult to find knowledge and interests within their

46

experience through which the intentions of the unit could be achieved. Oral activities using a tape-recorder could replace writing for those who would have great difficulty in written work. There is also a tape intended to form the basis of the teacher's own collection of spoken material. Some parts relate to particular units, while others can be used with several units.

As the above outline indicates, the aim of the project is to enable pupils to explore their own experience of language – to develop an awareness of what language is, how it is used and in using it to extend their competence in speaking and writing.

To some teachers of disadvantaged children this may appear ambitious, perhaps even unrealistic, in view of the language limitations of their pupils. But, as the authors point out, even if pupils appear to have difficulty in meeting the linguistic demands of school, they do have quite an extensive experience of language – for example, their own everyday experience, experience of sports commentators, advertisers, technical language and special languages such as those of disc jockeys and teenage groups, etc. They are not unaware of the variety in language and its uses; much more could be done to develop their awareness from this basis of personal experience. It is the view of the project team that the development of awareness will have a positive, though perhaps indirect, effect upon the pupil's competence. A more direct contribution to competence comes from the activities in the units – discussion in small groups, improvised and scripted acting, writing directed to a specific task which arises out of small group discussion and is then subject to comment by other members of the class.

It is a fundamental feature of the material that 'what is done with it must depend upon the teachers who use it.' A glance through the material will immediately suggest certain themes and units which seem likely to be attractive and relevant to particular groups, or which suggest interesting adaptations. For a starting point with slow learners, some suggestions are made at the end, based on wide experience in the classroom during the trial period.

One important advantage of the material is that it will often give the teacher himself a new awareness and understanding of language which should help to create a genuine sense of mutual exploration.

Summary

Language in Use, with its emphasis on starting within pupils' own experience of language, on oral work and group participation, seems very appropriate to the needs of slow learners. Many of the suggestions are immediately applicable to slow learners and it would not be difficult to adapt others to suit the interests and competence of particular groups.

The notion that pupils should be helped to become more aware of language – its functions and, in an elementary way, how it develops for particular purposes – is an important one for slow learners. For example, they should realize that language varies according to the social situation (e.g. telephoning, interviews, taking messages, conversation). This aspect of competence should be considered as much as vocabulary growth, comprehension and expression. However, there is much in *Language in Use* which should help directly to promote vocabulary and to facilitate genuine and involved use of the mother tongue. (See Appendix B for details of other materials.)

Scope (English for Immigrant Children)

Materials developed by this project have become very well known and are in use in a great variety of educational establishments. The project (1966–71) was based at the University of Leeds and organized by June Derrick.

Materials have been developed in four main areas, and there is a series of handbooks dealing with general aspects of immigrant education. The materials are published by Longman. At the time of the survey only *Scope*, Stage 1 – *An Introductory English Course for Immigrant Children* had been published. The starting point is spoken English, leading to reading and writing. This course is built around fourteen topics, both in the oral and in the reading and writing materials. Reference is made to a group of children and their families – of mixed ethnic origin – living in King Street. The topics and the theme of the King Street children and their families provide a focus of interest for the language scheme and for the eight readers. Children are given the opportunity to learn vocabulary and language structures which it is expected they will need in everyday situations.

The fourteen topics are: the classroom, shopping, family and home, stories, the fire, animals, the post office, King Street, the park, clothes, seeing the doctor, an island, farm animals and farming, the railway station.

There is considerable emphasis on the structural patterns of English. A detailed *Teacher's Book* is regarded by the authors as the key to the course. The materials provided include cut-out figures for use on magnet boards to help children recognize and talk about familiar objects and situations; there are flash cards, word cards, work books, picture cards and wall pictures and a record. The magnet board and figures are central to many activities. It is thought that most children require at least two terms to master the language in the course but it is recognized that teachers will have to adapt the pace of work to local requirements and to the particular situation in which they find themselves working. The materials are designed to be as flexible in use as possible so that teachers in reception centres, who may be able to spend a great deal of time on practice activities with the children, will be able to use *Scope* as readily as teachers in withdrawal classes. The latter will probably have to be more selective and after a brief, initial teaching period with one class, may have to divide the children into groups at different stages of progress.

Summary

We have observed *Scope*, Stage 1 in use in a great variety of teaching situations, have received reports from numerous teachers and have had personal experience of teaching with the materials. The scheme is recommended to any school faced with a proportion of non-English-speaking children. It is not limited to Asian communities though there is much emphasis on this group. Although primarily intended for the age group 8 to 13, it is possible to adapt the materials for use with older pupils. There is naturally some difficulty with some of the items which appeal more directly to the younger child. When all necessary reservations have been made about *Scope*, Stage 1 (and even with material produced in so determinedly empirical a fashion, there must naturally be some items which create disagreement), the team has produced a magnificent course which goes very far towards meeting the needs of this group of children in their period of initial learning of the English language.

Scope, Stage 2 and Senior Course

Most of this material was published in 1972.

Scope, Stage 2 – *A Language Development Course* was designed for use in multiracial classes with children in the middle-school age range, and offers language development work for both the immigrant and non-immigrant alike. Again, materials are arranged under themes: 'Homes', 'Water' and 'Travel' and consist of a *Teacher's Book*, separate pupils' books and a set of work cards for each theme. The *Teacher's Book* is regarded as an essential guide to the course; it examines the language problems in multiracial classes, and offers an approach to meet them. It gives detailed suggestions for the use of the pupils' books and work cards, lists language and vocabulary, provides guidance in language teaching techniques for use in the context of general class teaching and helps with class organization where levels of ability and language development vary considerably.

Scope Senior Course is intended for recently arrived, non-English-speaking immigrant pupils aged 14 or over. It is known that such pupils differ widely in ability and educational attainment – whereas some may already be able to read English, others are complete beginners and may be illiterate in their own language and in English. The *Senior Course* provides materials consisting of two teacher's books, three pupils' books, a work book, a set of wall pictures and two tapes. It is also intended that some items from *Scope*, Stage 1 will be included for those pupils who are unable to read or write. The pupils' books are entitled *We Live in England, Out and About in England* and *Ready for Work*.

Ready for Work covers ground somewhat similar to that described in the North West Regional Curriculum Development Project's Social Education materials. It has sections such as: 'The Careers Officer comes to the school', 'Have you thought about a job?', 'What do you do in your spare time?', 'Please write or phone', and gives advice about interviews. Numerous illustrations attempt to represent the leaving class at 'Shields Secondary School'. One topic opens with a picture of an attractive 15-year-old girl saying 'Hallo, my name's Vanessa Wolf', and other members of the class are introduced in similar terms. In the exercise simple questions are asked, 'What's Vanessa's surname?', 'What's Philip's middle name?' Exercise 3 asks about apostrophe 's'. Topic 2 deals with Hargit Singh Gill and his introduction to Vanessa. Exercise 6 gives part of Form 5B's timetable and the class is invited to answer Hargit's questions. By the time Section 6 is reached, the pupils are being asked to weigh the pros and cons of jobs which they might want to do.

Tina: Yes I *am* going to work in a factory! I like working with my hands and making things. It's easy for me. I don't want a job where I'd have to concentrate. I like to feel free to think about things that interest me.

Vanessa: But it'd be so boring! Making the same thing hour after hour, day after day . . .

Tina: Well, it'd drive me mad to walk into some job where I might make a fool of myself. I'm good at needlework so I'm pretty sure I wouldn't make a lot of mistakes . . .

Summary

The language, especially the vocabulary and the emphasis on certain sentence patterns, makes this material very suitable for disadvantaged children. There can be no doubt that the *Senior Course* will be very useful in remedial classes and departments, whether they contain a predominance of immigrant children or not.

Concept 7–9

Concept 7–9 is a course in language development, the result of a six-year project, Teaching English to West Indian Children (1967–73), based at the University of Birmingham. The materials have been widely tested in schools, and the project has considered the educational needs of children at the junior period in the light of recent thinking in both linguistics and curriculum theory. The materials have been designed to help children to develop those skills which underly success with language. Although designed to be of benefit to the whole range of ability at primary school, the materials have special relevance for schools where children come from educationally less favoured environments. Because the materials are concerned with basic language skills, they can usefully be applied in remedial situations with older children. The project, directed by Jim Wight (1967–72), assisted by F. J. Worsley (Director, 1972–73) and R. Norris, was set up initially to conduct research into the linguistic, social and emotional problems of West Indian children and to establish guidelines for the development of materials.

It quickly became apparent that the Creole languages so lovingly described by scholars were not in use by West Indian children in British classrooms, though they probably were in the playgrounds and in some homes. The West Indian children showed considerable efficiency in 'dialect code switching' and Jim Wight concluded that interference from Creole was not the sole, or even the major, reason for the children's poor performance at school. Although the West Indian dialect was found to impede progress in the children's learning of English in the areas of writing, spelling, oral comprehension, reading and intelligibility of speech, it appeared that the classroom language used by the children differed from standard English only to about the same extent as that of other strong dialect speakers – in rural Devon, say, or the Gorbals.

The implications of this discovery for the project were considerable. The materials produced aimed at improving the oral fluency and general communication skills of the children and only one unit was devoted to the correction of non-standard grammatical usages.

The materials

Concept 7–9 is published by E. J. Arnold. There is a variety of materials: specimen work books, spirit-duplicator masters, prompt-answer cards, pre-recorded cassettes, magnet cards, matrix cards, missing-picture books, symbol-drawing books, map-drawing books, 'where next?' game, route books, picture-matching books, detective-inquiry books, and teacher's manuals.

There are three closely interrelated units: Unit 1 – 'Listening with understanding', Unit 2 – 'Concept building', Unit 3 – 'Communication', and the Dialect Kit. The first unit seeks to improve the child's performance in listening skills. These are identified as attentiveness and concentration, memory, confidence and control, the ability to decode complex language, the ability to make deductions. Much of the material is presented on cassettes (and since the publishers market their own playback unit, it is this machine which is featured in the publicity material; however, cassettes are available for standard cassette players). The language in this unit is organized around six themes: (1) position; (2) what does it mean?; (3) what happens if?; (4) comparison; (5) the reason why; (6) time. As an example of the way in which the language is analysed, a summary of words and structures contained in lessons 30–35 of theme 6 is given. Among the structures employed are:

earlier/later/afterwards/the earliest
in the morning/afternoon/evening
at breakfast time/tea time, etc.
before somebody else/after somebody else
early in the morning
a few minutes later
x did something as soon as y happened/when y happened
x only did something after . . .
x is 5 years old . . . is the youngest.

The second unit, 'Concept building', aims to increase the children's skill and flexibility in classifying data. This unit is intended to be used by the whole class. The teaching is centred on the series of 'matrix' sheets – each matrix is a set of pictures arranged according to a number of significant groupings or classes. It is possible to arrange the pictures so that each row and each column of pictures forms a 'class'. In this way every picture belongs to a vertical and horizontal class.

The teaching procedure is for the teacher to introduce essential data on each new matrix, and a number of follow-up activities enable children individually or in groups to extend and reinforce their learning. Activity books have been provided, which start at the level of poor readers, and provide adequate cueing. The content of each matrix sheet has been chosen so that it can be used as a stimulus for a range of additional activities.

The 'Communication' unit is intended to increase skill in oral communication through activities that focus attention on the act of communication itself or, to put it more simply, to increase the children's oral skills of description and inquiry. A useful device is a free-standing partition with a posting-box aperture which can be set up between two children. One child instructs the other in the route to follow and his partner records the route on his symbol-drawing book, which enables the second child to judge the effectiveness of the first's description. Enjoyable games, such as 'detective inquiry' and 'treasure map', stimulate activities and enlarge the area of communication between the pair of children.

Finally, there is the Dialect Kit, intended specifically for West Indian children with dialectal difficulties. The kit is designed to counter the major effects of West Indian Creole dialects in writing standard English. A diagnostic test is included and the teacher's manual explains how the test is administered, and gives background information. This enables the teacher to identify extreme Creole speakers very readily. Although it remains true that most of the West Indian children will display facility in code-switching, some of the features which distinguish a Creole speaker from a standard English speaker are:

1. Marked plurals	di man-dem	The men
2. Marked past tense	mi en kom	I came
3. Inversion for emphasis	a sik Jan sik	John is *sick*
4. Unmarked plurals	three cup	three cups
5. Unmarked past tense	I never know	I never knew
6. Omission of verb 'to be'	John sick	John is sick
7. No subject–verb agreement	She have a cold	She has a cold
	The wind blow	The wind blows

Items 4 to 7 are the most likely sources of difficulty when it comes to the production of standard *written* forms. The project team emphasize that the materials should not be seen as an attack on the child's speech but rather as a means of helping him to be aware of the function of certain standard forms in a written context.

Summary

The activities have an immediate appeal to disadvantaged pupils and this is very apparent to anybody visiting a classroom where the materials are in use. The 'Listening with understanding' unit has the great advantage of being self-contained, so that the children are given activities which are independent of the teacher. There is no doubt that much of the material would have equal appeal to older disadvantaged pupils. Children over the age of 13 might baulk at certain of the devices adopted to amuse younger children, but much of this material is in cartoon style and has an appeal over a wide age range.

North West Regional Curriculum Development Project

The project was established in 1967 to study curriculum development in local centres, and to prepare materials for the raising of the school leaving age. It comprises a consortium of fifteen local development centres set up and maintained by thirteen LEAs; and it is controlled by a steering committee comprising teachers and LEA representatives. The work is co-ordinated through a regional centre, established in the University of Manchester School of Education, which was financed by the Schools Council. The director of the project is Dr W. G. A. Rudd. Materials have been developed by local teachers' groups and have been tested and revised after use in many schools.

The North West Regional Project sought to exemplify principles sketched out in Schools Council Working Paper No. 10, *Curriculum Development: Teachers' Groups and Centres* (HMSO, 1967).

In addition to developing new teaching materials for use with early-leaving pupils, the project has also been studying in detail the implications of two basic principles in curriculum development work in local centres:

a   that motive power should come primarily from local groups of teachers accessible one to another;
b   that there should be effective and close collaboration between teachers and all those who are able to offer co-operation.

Some of the English materials have been published (by Blackie) under the title *Situations: a Course in English*. There are two sections: section one for fourth-year pupils and section two for fifth-year pupils. It is claimed that each section contains enough materials for a teacher and class of up to thirty-five pupils.

At the time of writing, only section one was available. (Section two was published in 1973.) This contains a wallet of the teacher's *Situation* notes (fourteen main ones plus fifteen 'quickies'); nineteen wallets of pupils' material (each containing forty copies for class distribution); a specially recorded tape of songs, dramatizations, speech and sounds; a set of twenty colour slides; two packs of black and white photographs; a wallet of library work cards, and a teacher's guide. There are fourteen 'situations':

1. Fear
2. Conflict with parents
3. Quarrels between children
4. Feeling proud of your country
5. Leaving home to live one's own life
6. Admiration for others
7. Significance of sounds
8. Happy family relationships
9. Effect of strain on the family
10. Struggling with a sense of duty
11. Other people living in the family
12. Timing time

54

13. Boy meets girl
14. A day trip.

Then there is a series of activities under the title 'Observation and the senses'; there are no pupils' materials or audio-visual aids with this, merely teachers' situation notes for each of the eleven exercises, which are designed to sharpen the perception of common objects and experiences and to improve vocabulary. Titles include: Getting up, A visit to the barber's or hairdresser's, A meal, A do-it-yourself job.

Also provided are 'Names and descriptions', four 'quickies' on the use of language in advertising. The titles are: Cars, Cosmetics, Goods for sale, Jobs.

A list of forty recommended books for a class library is given in the *Teacher's Guide*. As far as possible the list is of paperback editions, in order to make books seem 'unscholastic and accessible'.

The course prides itself on taking a realistic view of the capabilities of pupils in the lower half of the ability and attainment range, and seeks to stimulate activities to a degree which will give the teacher a good opportunity to raise standards of attainment.

The *Teacher's Guide* is particularly good on discussion, giving a detailed breakdown of instructions on conducting a class discussion and a group discussion. The kind of practical bias may be illustrated by quoting the Guide's answer to groups which do not discuss well. It is suggested that the group should be re-arranged and that 'there are various ways of doing this: (*a*) by removing the dominant talkers (noted from previous discussion) and placing them in one group, so allowing the more timid to speak, (*b*) by making sure that friends are split and possibly "enemies" are placed together; and (*c*) by grouping the pupils according to their interests.' Discussion may be based on personal experience, vicarious experience or on the completion of questionnaires.

A section on drama has notes intended for teachers new to this work. The Guide is brief (perhaps over-brief) but readable and useful. Typical materials would consist of slides, photographs, taped puzzle sounds, a poem, cartoon, taped music and speech, taped reminiscences, an agony-column letter. Typical pupil activities would be imaginative writing, group discussion, filling in a question-naire, library research leading to group displays, a quiz, a written character study, group discussion of answers. To take one example in more detail: situation 4 – 'Feeling proud of your country'. The teacher is urged to have a tape-recorder and photographs ready and to have collected any additional suitable material. The only *essential* teaching material is the master tape and photographs, which are provided. The lesson is set out in simple form under three headings: 'Teaching material', 'Development' and 'Aims'. Opening with the master tape, which contains 'There'll always be an England', the national anthem and a crowd shouting 'England! England!', the development might include playing the taped extracts, showing the photographs, drawing the pupils' attention to any display the teacher has created, and conducting a short discussion. Some questions to start the discussion might be – 'Do you like living in this country or would you like to emigrate?', 'Do you stand when the national anthem is played?', 'Why?', 'Do you always shout for your country in national competitions?', 'Why?'.

Despite the avowed intention of keeping the material simple, the reading level of certain extracts seems to be rather demanding. For example, the extract from Keith Waterhouse's play, *There is a Happy Land*, would be usable only if the teacher were either to read it aloud or to put it on tape beforehand so that the pupils could hear it through. However, given this degree of preparation, the extract would be amusing and relevant.

The North West Regional Curriculum Development Project's Social Education materials are discussed on page 83. Other courses are being published. These include: Domestic Studies (Holmes McDougall) and Technology and Health courses published by the project itself. (At present these can be purchased from Mr W. Dempsey, Blackburn Teachers' Centre, St Paul's Avenue, Blackburn and Mr A. E. Arstall, Curriculum Development Centre, Flixton Road, Urmston, Lancashire, respectively.)

These materials contain much that is useful and usable by teachers of disadvantaged children and if they are not innovatory in the broadest sense, the project feels that they do represent a major offering from this group of teachers to their colleagues up and down the country who are currently facing similar problems.

The project has emphasized a 'client-centred' approach, based on organizing groups of teachers to tackle professional problems *identified by themselves*. The client-centred approach emphasizes individual and group autonomy. In a way, the products of the groups (though far from negligible) are less important than the 'process skills' the members acquire – skills which can be directed in the future towards other professional problems. This and the knowledge of how such groups could be organized, led and supported, was seen as the justification for the School of Education's investment in the client-centred approach to in-service education.

V. Humanities

Recent developments in humanities teaching

As recently as 1967, teaching in the humanities could be regarded in general as the least successful in our schools. During the succeeding five years, a number of Schools Council projects have been labouring to alter this situation. There has been a greater willingness to consider controversial topics and a greater determination to integrate subjects. Controversies in this area of the curriculum have been conducted publicly, with conviction and passion, and though they have sometimes generated more heat than light, the debate is, and has been, infinitely worth while.

Schools Council Working Paper No. 11, *Society and the Young School Leaver: a Humanities Programme in Preparation for the Raising of the School-leaving Age* (HMSO, 1967), pointed out that the schools which appeared to be making most progress put the needs and interests of the youngsters before the content of the course. The working paper contained a number of examples of 'experience-based learning' of the kind which is common in primary schools. These suggestions for projects are still worth looking at. They give practical details on how to begin and what to do. The approaches used drew upon the existing experience of schools whereas some of the more recent work, such as the Humanities Curriculum Project, breaks new ground both in terms of content and method.

It is hardly a source of wonder that teachers of the humanities are afflicted with some feelings of confusion. The tradition of teaching separate subjects still seems predominant in most secondary schools; the Schools Council itself has produced publications on the humanities called, *Humanities for the Young School Leaver – an Approach through History* (Evans/Methuen Educational, 1969) and *Humanities for the Young School Leaver – an Approach through English* (HMSO, 1968). Working Paper No. 11, however, suggested that 'the ultimate goal is an integrated syllabus in the humanities, not in order to create a new subject of doubtful parentage, but to lay all the old subjects, and many of the newer disciplines, under tribute to answer real questions in which the pupils can be interested.'

The work of those projects which have sought to achieve an integration of subject matter within the humanities has been complicated, not only by the practical difficulties, but also by the lack of a theoretical framework which is broadly agreed by teachers. 'Integration' is a term widely used by humanities teams but with a variety of meanings. David Bolam, Director of the Schools Council Integrated Studies Project (1968–72) based at the University of Keele, interpreted it to mean the exploration of any large area, theme or problem which (a) requires the help of more than one subject discipline for its full understanding; (b) is best taught by the concerted action of a team of teachers. Pat Logan has worked with a team of sixteen teachers at Henbury School, Bristol, and has been 'doing integrated studies in history, geography and religious education in up to twenty mixed-ability groups in the first two years of school . . . The aim of the team has been to create in the pupils a lively awareness of their total environment. This has been done by retaining the fundamental concepts of the separate disciplines but presenting them without the isolating constraints of subject barriers. The team has emphasized the need for pupils to take some responsibility for their own learning, and has attempted to build a degree of flexibility into the programme so that it is suitable for the individual needs of all pupils. To this end there has been much encouragement of co-operative work in small groups.'*

Rex Beddis and Thomas Dalton, Directors of the Schools Council Geography for the Young School Leaver Project (1970–74), based at Avery Hill College of Education in London, firmly support geography as a discipline in its own right. Geography, faced like other disciplines with an explosion of knowledge and its rapid obsolescence, has had to examine the framework of concepts and knowledge within which its exponents must work. 'This has expressed itself in the need to crystallize information into cores of understanding, to search for order and pattern in the location of human activity and a consequent desire to be more precise and objective in measurement and analysis. There is an increasing emphasis on man's role in society – the social implications.'†

Geography, in this broad sense, can help to develop valuable skills and attitudes in the young school leaver. The project team's view is that there are a number of issues and problems of real concern to all young people. No single subject can adequately explain and analyse them but each specialism may have a unique contribution to make in their understanding. This does not involve any loss of identity for the specialist teacher or the subject. Indeed, the subject may gain in stature through being seen to be valuable in the consideration of significant issues, and in focusing attention on the central ideas of the subject.

The Humanities Curriculum Project (1967–72) was set up as part of the Schools Council's programme for the young school leaver. The project's director was L. A. Stenhouse, and the project based at the University of East Anglia (1970–72). The project committed itself, quite simply, to inquiry-based courses which cross the traditional boundaries between English, history, geography, religious

---

* *Team Teaching in Integrated Studies*, Henbury Comprehensive School, Bristol.
† Teacher's guide to Theme 1, '*Man, Land and Leisure*' (Nelson, 1974).

studies and social studies. It followed the well-tried thematic approach, and developed collections of materials around such themes as education, the family, poverty, etc. These have been published by Heinemann Educational Books.

There is much to be said for an integration of subjects in the education of disadvantaged children, and certainly of slow-learning children. Integration is likely to bring out the broad themes which they can understand and respond to, and their learning is less likely to be fragmented and unrelated. They probably gain less from the presentation of a sequence of ideas than from the opportunity to deepen their understanding of a few major topics and areas, and the projects discussed below seem to be adopting a sensible view of their subject matter and of the kind of organization which will be required to put their schemes into effect with disadvantaged pupils. Beyond this, their achievements vary considerably so far as our population is concerned. There is a great deal left to do.

Social Education Project

This three-year project, director Professor H. Davies, was organized by John Rennie, and based at the University of Nottingham. It completed its work in 1971. It produced no teaching materials since it wished to draw attention to social education as a *process* rather than as a subject with a specific content – a process through which groups of children acquire social skills and develop social awareness in the course of undertaking their own chosen inquiries. The report of the project has been published as Schools Council Working Paper 51, *Social Education: an Experiment in Four Secondary Schools* (Evans/Methuen Educational, 1974).

The project team viewed social education as an enabling process through which children might acquire skills which would allow them both to achieve greater understanding of society and to effect changes within it. There are three kinds of skills which social education can help children to attain.

1 *Skills of observation and communication*

Children need help to observe and to become more aware, both in ordinary relationships and in wider social situations. Help is also needed to develop the ability to communicate in different situations and groups, and this is an even more important element in human relationships.

2 *Analytic and diagnostic skills*

By means of profiles (studies of their class, their area, particular institutions)

59

children can look in depth at structures and groups which have an immediate impact upon them. As a result of these inquiries, children may wish to suggest changes and to take action to help in some way or to improve a situation. The difference between this and community service may be that the children have themselves become aware of a need and have attempted to plan a solution.

3 *Social skills*

It is apparent that to undertake such profiles, whether simple ones within the school or more sophisticated ones in the community, pupils need to acquire certain skills. (For many disadvantaged and slow-learning children, this process would itself constitute valuable learning apart from any insights derived from the completed profiles.) Some of these social skills are:

a   willingness to approach others
b   willingness to ask relevant questions and ability to do so
c   avoidance of off-putting questions and remarks
d   willingness to insert questions and remarks designed to put people at their ease
e   lack of undue inhibitions – willingness and ability to answer relevantly and simply questions about self
f   making practical suggestions to initiate group action
g   accepting such suggestions from others
h   collaborating in group projects
i   leadership in group projects.

Socio-drama

The Social Education Project, like the Moral Education Project, attached particular importance to role-playing or socio-drama – the improvised dramatization of specific social situations – as a means of developing these skills of awareness and communication. Through socio-drama, children can learn to notice what is significant in social events, to interpret behaviour and communications and to understand and communicate their own feelings and reactions.

The project team recognized that socio-drama is often difficult to get going and that some teachers lack confidence to attempt it. They advocate, therefore, a systematic building-up of experience and skill in the use of socio-drama. Their graded suggestions are a useful source of ideas; the teacher would need to judge what stage would be an appropriate starting point for a particular class.

Their system begins with mimes of simple expressive feelings:

Come here (I am angry with you)
Come here (I have something to show you)
Fear (in a dark room)
Terror (attacked by a vicious dog)
Wonderful news
Surprise.

The next stage might involve the miming of everyday situations (pouring tea, making a bed, brushing teeth, etc.) until it is felt that group situations can be presented in which pupils are encouraged to show feeling and consideration for others:

Crowd on bus (who gives up seat for old person?)
Crowd crossing street (who will help child or old person?)
Fight in street (help for wounded or injured man)
People in flat (who will find out or inquire if the old lady is all right?)
Crowd at bus stop (suddenly it starts raining; small children and old person in queue).

Situation 'tests' can be introduced once simple drama is going reasonably well. Situations can be described on slips of paper and distributed to the groups for them to act them out. The situations are simple at first, but later pose complex questions and may introduce, for example, a family in which brother and sister have conflicting interests, with father, mother and perhaps even grandparents becoming involved. Eventually, situations like these may be attempted:

An immigrant family moves into the area. The son comes to your youth club and falls into an argument with one of your friends.

Father insists that you come in at ten o'clock but allows your older brother to stay out later.

A neighbour asks you to look after her children while she visits her husband in hospital. You have promised to go out with your friends.

Starting work, you are picked on by a boy who started last year. The foreman sees him, but seems to ignore it.

Profiles

An important feature of the approach are profiles or studies of social groups – the class, the school, the peer group, and ultimately the local community. The aspects to be studied are chosen and developed by the children and may well lead on to further profiles. The class profiles might include, for example, such items as

61

where pupils live, pocket money, favourite television programmes, holidays of class members, etc. A school profile might look at duties and responsibilities of people in the school, attitudes of members of the school and of people in the community towards the school. Area profiles might be concerned with a wide range of issues in the neighbourhood and community, its facilities, services and problems. The aim of the profiles is not just to gather information but to practise specific social skills and to develop understanding, insight and, ultimately, concern.

The techniques used may involve tape-recording, photography, model-making, diagrams, maps, graphs, creative writing, drawing and painting, as well as socio-drama and discussion. The range of activities increases the chances of an academically weak child being able to participate successfully in some way or other – and the emphasis on pupils' responsibility and activity should help to ensure motivation.

Clearly, the project's view of the process of social education entails giving more responsibility for choices and decisions to the children. The teacher in this situation is less of an information-giver and disciplinarian and more a member of the group – a senior colleague working with junior colleagues, as it were. This does not mean a permissive classroom but one where co-operation and mutual agreement are part of the process of social education. Difficult though this can be, it is the right educative and therapeutic experience for disadvantaged children, and if slow learners appear not to have the ability and capacity for it that is all the more reason for making a start on it. The gradual initiation into the use of socio-drama would be a good beginning.

It is interesting that in the schools involved in the work of the project, the pupils engaged in social education were taken from the lowest ability groups. An initial problem was their lack of confidence and unwillingness to show initiative which resulted from their academic failure. The project team attempted to combat this by encouraging the children to realize that intelligence is displayed not only in abstract or technical learning but also in creativeness and social intelligence – the ability to understand people and relationships.

While working on area profiles, children often develop specific interests and undertake area surveys in relation to these. Thus they undertake not only wide-ranging surveys but also quite specific in-depth inquiries into a particular aspect of their community. From such work it is hoped that pupils will develop the sense of identification which will lead them to decide to become involved in their community. In the project schools, the most spectacular kind of involvement occurred in a city-centre school in a redevelopment area. The pupils produced their own alternative redevelopment plan, showing a level of sophistication and invention which was a revelation to planners, councillors and, not least, their teachers.

Other schools became involved in local nursery schools and in producing pamphlets for local contributory primary schools. All these kinds of involvement arose from decisions taken by the children themselves.

Humanities Curriculum Project

The Social Education Project did not avoid controversial issues but in setting its face against the production of teaching materials, it avoided public controversy as to its intentions, aims and objectives. This has certainly not been the case with the Humanities Curriculum Project. From the beginning, it sought to grapple with the problem of dealing with areas of study which involve highly controversial, social, ethical or political values. The project's short definition of a controversial issue was: one which divides teachers, pupils and parents.

The Humanities Curriculum Project decided to explore the problems of teaching controversial subjects by adopting nine themes or topics for experimental development. These were: War and society, Education, The family, Relations between the sexes, People and work, Poverty, Living in cities, Law and order, and Race. Collections, or packs, of materials on all these themes had been published at the time of writing, with the exception of the 'Race' pack (which will not now be published). There can be no doubt that, at every level, the Humanities Curriculum Project has provoked discussion. To some extent this must enter into one's assessment of the material's efficacy. To adopt the Humanities Curriculum Project is, for the head of a school, to take a step rather different in kind from that involved in adopting, say, Nuffield Science.

Schools Council Working Paper No. 2, *Raising the School Leaving Age: a Co-operative Programme of Research and Development* (HMSO, 1965), suggested that the aim of humanities projects was to forward understanding, discrimination and judgement. The Humanities Curriculum Project assumed that full understanding implied the capacity for discrimination and judgement. The aim was to develop understanding of the nature and structure of certain complex value issues of universal human concern.

This aim seems as valid for disadvantaged children as for any others. Even though they may not be able to bring to the discussion of such issues the powers of reasoning, the verbal fluency and the familiarity with ideas which intelligent children from more favoured homes are able to do, they share with other adolescents the need to develop a view of life, to test their opinions in conversation and to become more aware of other people's points of view. While they lack some kinds of experience, they may well have other personal experience relevant to some of the issues raised in the project materials – as was obvious in some of the reports we received.

63

The materials and methods of the Humanities Curriculum Project

The essence of the approach is discussion in small groups, and an important feature is that the teacher functions as a neutral chairman. Collections of materials are available as evidence which can be drawn upon at the beginning of or during the discussion.

The basis, aims, procedures and techniques of the project are outlined in *The Humanities Project: an Introduction*. It does not offer a set scheme; it is not a syllabus; rather is it 'a programme of continuing research and development', and its aim is 'to make it possible for a large number of teachers to mount in their own schools experimental programmes of research and development on the platform of the experience gathered by the Project' (page 1). To this end, the Humanities Project sought to integrate the arts, religion, history, social sciences and ethics, and to study certain major controversial issues by a discussion method.

For each of these issues the project planned to publish a 'foundation collection' of printed and audio-visual materials which could be supplemented by pupils' research or from other sources. The printed materials were obtained from a wide variety of sources and include poems and songs; extracts from drama, novels and biography; letters, reports, articles; readings from the social sciences; maps, cartoons, questionnaires, advertisements and photographs. These are stored in a convenient pack and are intended to be drawn on by the teacher for evidence as the discussion continues. Each collection contains twenty copies of each of 200 pieces of printed material – each twenty in a polythene bag. The pack also includes two copies of the introduction booklet, a set of tapes and two teachers' sets, each containing one copy of each piece of printed material and one copy of the handbook on the area of inquiry (including synopses of approximately 100 recommended films).

Use of the materials with disadvantaged pupils

The Humanities Project: an Introduction states that it was the intention of the project to offer teaching materials and research support to teachers working with adolescents of average and below-average ability (IQ range 70–110). Pupils in need of remedial reading were specifically excluded (page 6). However, there are many pupils – particularly in the below-average range – who are limited in reading ability and verbal comprehension.

The difficulty level of the materials was an initial problem, reflected in many of the reports we received:

Secondary modern school, Norfolk
This material is being used with the fourth-year class of mixed-ability groups, each of which includes the disadvantaged children. The teachers are still experimenting with the materials. There is a general impression that the materials are too difficult for disadvantaged pupils without considerable modification; many do not have the required reading ability.

Non-selective secondary school, Worcestershire
The main concern here is that the language and concept level of much of the material is too difficult and abstract for the lowest-ability children to understand.

Village college, Cambridgeshire
We found it necessary to be very selective with these pupils. Some of the material was too difficult for the majority.

Non-selective school, Surrey
The vocabulary is generally outside the range of most of the pupils we have used the material with.

A Yorkshire comprehensive
Although discussion in addition to reading assists student understanding, we still find in some of the materials that the vocabulary is very difficult, the ideas too complex, the passages too dull, and that some of the material soon dates.

Dissertation at Hull College of Education
The findings of the 'Words Concepts' test, the analysis of the reading material and teachers' opinions, lead us to the conclusion that too high an expectation of fourth-year leavers' power of comprehension is possibly entertained both by teachers and the compilers of the material.

Dissertation at Maria Grey College of Education
The teacher using HCP considered that a reading age of about 11+ was required before a pupil could really play a part in using the material.

However, this is by no means the whole story and we received many reports indicating successful, even enthusiastic, use. It should be pointed out that the collections include pictorial and taped material and it is also possible for teachers and pupils to develop their own collections of evidence. We wondered whether it would not be feasible to prepare collections of evidence which were more suited to slower and less able pupils.

The Humanities Curriculum Project evaluators have found a strong link between teacher effectiveness and attendance at a training course, and most of those whom we saw using the materials with pleasure and success had taken part in such courses, as well as having spent much of their own time mastering their resources. These collections represent an ambitious attempt to provide ready-to-hand resources for the busy teacher. Not surprisingly, many have found this richness a mixed blessing, since the task of familiarizing oneself with so much material (to 'crack the pack' as the initiated expressed it) is a considerable one. It cannot escape the notice of anyone who looks seriously at the provision of additional resources that, far from easing the teacher's lot, they greatly intensify the demands on his time and energy. However, the rewards should follow from greater pupil involvement, a diminution of discipline problems, an altogether more pleasant working atmosphere and, in due course, a higher quality of school performance. These were, indeed, the consequences some schools recorded.

High school, Isle of Wight
We have our fourth year working on team-teaching methods. The material is selected and adapted (it is so full) but the scheme is a great success. Staff, including those who have not taught the least able before, are most enthusiastic and it is having a spill-over effect on other groups and subjects.

Secondary modern school, Midlands conurbation
The headteacher was most enthusiastic about the HCP which he felt had transformed the teaching of some members of staff. He reiterated again and again the advantages of returning to the 'evidence'; this seemed to him to be the key to the whole method, as one was not relying upon uninformed opinion but had before one printed or visual evidence and the discussion must concentrate on this so that opinions would grow from it.

Comprehensive school, Isle of Wight
Beyond doubt *some* of the material in every pack is far too difficult for the educationally disadvantaged but by careful selection suitable material could be found. Much of the jargon relating to sociology, for example, is a stumbling block but the pictures, tapes, films, cartoons, newspaper extracts, ensure that the disadvantaged are not precluded from discussion. One of the major problems being faced here is the inability of many children to articulate their thoughts and opinions and this applies to others as well as the educationally disadvantaged; but this should grow out as the primary and middle schools continue to encourage their pupils to express themselves more freely orally and in writing. The material is so varied in kind and standard of difficulty that the composition of the groups using it assumes considerable importance. We are using a fairly wide range of ability with the fourth year,

66

a narrower range with the fifth-year groups. With the latter, things are going very well, less so with the younger pupils – possibly because the pupils are less mature, particularly the socially and educationally disadvantaged.

Other teachers had made modifications to the original materials or had blended them with their own. Films, pictures, extracts from novels, extracts from popular newspapers and even some additional poems had been incorporated. Finding that certain material dated quickly, a Cheshire secondary school asked the pupils to bring their own and the whole class had become great newspaper readers: 'we have had more success with the least able children than with the others.' A boys' secondary school in Devon summed up the attitude that would allow teachers to make something of the Humanities Project materials:

> By no means all of the material is suitable for groups with less than average ability but I have not found any lack of suitable material.

There is a great deal of non-verbal material, and judicious selection allowed most pupils to take part if the teacher began with the conviction that this was possible. Some groups we visited were certainly very dull. A number of people have measured the duration of the pauses in the discussions, and concluded that oral discussion with disadvantaged pupils is doomed to failure. We are far from convinced that this need be the case. A number of schools claimed that the material was *more* successful with less able children because (*a*) talking is easier than writing; (*b*) 'our bright children took a long time to loosen up – they have been taught traditionally.'

Obviously, skill in discussion and the consideration of ideas is not something that can be suddenly acquired. It depends on previous experience of oral language work and also on the atmosphere and teacher–pupil relationships in school. One perhaps needs to think in terms of 'readiness' for the Humanities Project approach, with previous preparation for it comparable to the step-by-step preparation for socio-drama proposed by the Social Education Project. Oral language work should begin early in the children's school lives. It should be organized talk, and systematically developed around themes which are interesting to pupils of a particular age group. With the growth of CSE Mode III courses, many schools are now entering candidates for Oral English, so that this aspect of language teaching no longer requires defending; a number of schools had based a syllabus on the Humanities Curriculum Project.

It appeared that all the collections appealed to some group. A Hull secondary modern school had found the 'Family' pack most rewarding, and the 'War and society' pack the least rewarding; a Monmouthshire secondary modern school had made most headway with 'War and society', least with 'Family'. A Paignton school liked 'Family' best, a Middlesborough school had found it 'of limited use'. Between them, schools who returned questionnaires had used, in addition to the two packs mentioned, 'Education', 'Relations between the sexes', 'People and work', 'Law and order' and 'Poverty'.

One teacher pointed out that the materials provide for other activities besides discussion. 'What work is undertaken is largely controlled by the pupils, who take part together with the chairman, in producing an agenda for the discussion and activities. It is they who decide the important themes or points of interest.' Another teacher said that a 'sense of tolerance' had developed, while the boys and girls had increased their social confidence: 'there is the chance to express oneself and succeed, which is important for slow learners.' A third expressed these views:

> I feel that what is necessary is a sympathy for the inquiry method throughout the school. It needs to start in the first, second and third year, then when you come to use the HCP, the children are ready for it. This I feel strongly: the inquiry method is truly a learning situation. It has a great humanizing effect upon both children and staff. The impact of the material is just as great on the teacher as on the pupil. I believe strongly that it is socially advantageous to the slow learners.

There can be no doubt that the Humanities Curriculum Project material acts on the teacher as well as on the pupil. One teacher said that in eighteen years of experience no other lessons had worried him as much as these *because the outcome was unpredictable.* He liked to know what would happen, to be in charge. He was critical of the project. The less able child was unable to think in the way that the evidence wished him to; the more able pupils were not keen on helping the less able as it was proposed they would. The mechanics of reading defeated many of the less able who were not, therefore, in a position to take advantage of the evidence. It took so long for them to work through the reading matter that the more able became bored. Also, reading the evidence seemed to be an unsuccessful ploy in that it broke the thread of discussion if, by some chance, this had become animated.

These preliminary remarks prepared one for a dull and somewhat unproductive oral session. It was at a school where the pupils stood when a visitor entered the room and where each sentence was completed by 'Sir'. Corporal punishment was used – most masters kept a slipper to administer their own corporal punishment as required. This must obviously be a factor in the discussions about any of the themes, but especially when the 'Education' pack is used and immediately introduces questions of sanctions and invites open discussion. It really is venturesome to introduce controversial topics directly relating to everyday events. The outcome is, indeed, unpredictable and in a class where one's hold was somewhat tenuous and dependent on physical sanctions, it would clearly be dangerous to open the situation in this way.

This was a point which had not been fully grasped in another large school we visited. The school obviously took pride in the high standards of work attained by its examination streams. There was no impression that the less able were rejected by the school but it was fairly clear to these pupils that they did not enjoy the same status as those preparing for GCE or CSE. The school operated a system of streaming. The leavers' class was formed at the end of the third year from all those pupils not taking an examination, whichever class they had previously occupied, and once constituted it took all its lessons as a separate unit except for some practical work and games. Arrangements were made in the first two years for systematic remedial work to be undertaken in the lowest of three ability bands; pupils were allocated to these bands after a battery of tests administered soon after their arrival in the secondary school. Within the lowest band, a withdrawal group system operated, and it was claimed that by the end of the second year, most pupils' severe learning disabilities had been met – so much so that the teacher in charge of remedial work felt that it was the B stream whose needs were more likely to have been neglected.

The school had replied to our questionnaire about the Humanities Curriculum Project as follows:

> The main concern here is that the language and concept level of much of the material is too difficult and abstract for the lowest ability children to understand.
> The limited experiences of the children tend to make them less responsive in free discussion and the teacher is tempted to 'teach' rather than remain neutral as chairman.

When observed, the leavers' class was making use of the 'Family' pack. They were writing plays, working in groups of four or five. This was a more formal presentation of material which had previously been worked out by the boys and girls in conversation groups. One group then acted their play, taking the roles of father, mother and daughter. The boy depicted a rigid, authoritarian personality with some success. The dialogue presented a conflict situation (staying out late) between the father and daughter; the latter then attempted to play off the more permissive mother against the repressive father. The mother's speech-making was confined to saying 'Yes' and it was obvious that a great deal of work would be required in order to produce any kind of coherent statement. Even so, it was apparent that the concepts in this section of the material were fully appropriate to these lowest ability pupils. The teacher commented, however, that the reading level was above that attained by many of them, despite the good progress noted above.

This teacher admitted that he was new to the work and introduced it in a rather apologetic manner which naturally affected the pupils' attitudes. What was being done seemed, within these limitations, very worth while and capable of further development but, and the teacher saw this himself, the project's philosophy, with its emphasis upon the individual and the examined life, inevitably produces sharp differences of opinion among a large staff. The head, keen to keep abreast of innovations, was equally determined to maintain the formal structure which had brought his school good examination results and prestige in the neighbourhood: when these low-status children began to ask questions, or to comment on the school as a social institution as encouraged by project material, the head might, the teacher felt, withdraw his support.

This lesson had illustrated a variant on the discussion method. We also saw interesting art work, sculpture, poetry and other creative writing derived from the project. Nevertheless, the core of the approach is group discussion; a more 'orthodox' lesson was observed in another school.

This school was using 'Relations between the sexes'. There were six boys and six girls in the group, all of these were fifth-years. We observed two sessions with this group.

At the first session a film on the Pilgrim Homes was shown. This showed a child in care and the circumstances leading to this. After the film, the students formed a circle, and it was noticeable that this group did not split solely into boy–girl groupings. The order of the circle was in threes – three boys, then three girls, etc. The teacher sat between two of these groups.

The film was discussed, the chairman starting the discussion by asking for comments on a particular aspect. This discussion was orderly, and the children listened to each other's opinions. There were silences which were not interrupted by the chairman. Sometimes the chairman drew a certain child into the discussion by asking his opinion. From the observation, we felt that the whole discussion, although not reaching a high level of thinking, was relevant and allowed the children to express their own ideas.

At the second session a number of pieces of evidence were handed to the children; these were:

    1578   Marriage and procreation
    1596   Matrimonial harmonics
    1595   Harmony before matrimony
    1578   A viewpoint on marriage.

Two of these (1596, 1595) were Hogarthian cartoons. The students were given time to examine or read the evidence. Then discussion was started around the cartoons – was marriage really like this?

The discussion at some stages reached a fairly high level and again it was orderly and the chairman remained neutral. Into this discussion came the personal involvement. One girl had a sister who had separated from her husband and this was brought into the discussion by the girl. The chairman was skilful at drawing children into discussion but was careful not to commit himself or influence the proceedings. We got the impression that we were observing the use of the material as expected by the HCP project team. It is to be noted that this teacher had attended the HCP course.

The idea of neutrality

This aspect of the Humanities Curriculum Project has attracted a good deal of attention, so much so that P. Wenham could write:

> In the long run it may well prove that the most significant contribution of the project to curriculum development lies in the method rather than the materials.*

Lawrence Stenhouse certainly regarded neutrality as a central issue in the early days of the project.† His article, 'Open-minded teaching' in *New Society*‡ appeared with the sub-title: 'Will the role of teacher in future be much more like that of the impartial judge? Instead of putting across opinions he will help in a weighing of evidence.' Stenhouse stated his position again, with a slightly different emphasis, towards the end of the project, in his article, 'The idea of neutrality'.§

It is claimed by the project's evaluators that shifts in pupils' attitude show statistical significance in favour of those groups where the chairman has maintained neutrality. Nevertheless, many teachers have remained unconvinced: 'most, indeed, feel that neutral chairmanship, the core of the HCP approach, is undesirable; that it conflicts with personal teaching styles and the teacher's commitment to moral values in the classroom.'||

As far as the disadvantaged are concerned, we feel that the teacher must be

* 'Humanities: problems in the package', *Resources*, February 1972.
† L. A. Stenhouse, 'Handling controversial issues in the classroom', *Education Canada*, December 1969.
‡ 24 July 1969.
§ *Times Educational Supplement*, 4 February 1972.
|| L. A. Stenhouse, 'Open-minded teaching'.

free to intervene, to stimulate, to vary the discussion, to introduce activities. This is not by any means to say that the idea of neutrality has nothing to offer. Many of the themes suggested by the project could never be tackled if the teacher could not maintain impartiality – the term now favoured by the project. It is a useful discipline for the teacher to train himself not to intervene too readily but to wait patiently while a pupil struggles for self-expression. But the discussion group with its committee atmosphere is a sophisticated form of discussion which disadvantaged children may not take to easily. Given a measure of flexibility and competence on the teacher's part, it is not so difficult to organize informal talk and discussion which, as well as drawing upon the collections of evidence, makes greater use of a diversity of experience – tapes of incidents, recorded extracts from stories and newspapers, films, slides, television programmes and dramatization.

Conclusions

1 We are convinced of the importance of this kind of work for disadvantaged children and that the opportunity for frank, orderly and systematic discussion of adult issues is highly desirable.

2 The Humanities Curriculum Project approach is not a simple undertaking even with average children. If it is to have a fair trial, it is important for teachers to be well briefed in the aims and methods of the project, preferably by attending a training course.

3 It was widely agreed by teachers that many disadvantaged pupils would have difficulty in using the printed material either because their reading attainment was inadequate or because the style and the ideas of the passages were too demanding.

4 Despite this, many schools were making enthusiastic use of selected materials, especially those not requiring reading, or were supplementing the collections with materials of their own choosing.

5 We recommend that some of those concerned with disadvantaged children might prepare collections of pictorial and audio-visual material better suited to the least successful pupils in secondary schools.

6 The successful use of the Humanities Project approach must depend, particularly in the case of disadvantaged children, on previous experience of oral language work, discussion, and consideration of social issues at a simpler level. The Moral Education Project materials, for example, would provide a good preparation for using the Humanities Project with an older age group.

7 We consider that the ideal of the teacher as a neutral chairman is an

72

important one (perhaps especially so with children whose social and cultural backgrounds are likely to be diverse and different from that of the teacher). We think, however, that the teacher of children who tend to be rather inarticulate and who do not find it easy to handle ideas should not feel himself inhibited and constrained by this ideal. He must surely adopt a flexible approach to the means of initiating and sustaining discussion. Similarly, there is no obligation to accept the formal discussion group as the only form of classroom organization.

Integrated Studies Project

This project, based at the University of Keele and directed by David Bolam, was established to explore the problems and possibilities of integrated humanities courses during the first four years of secondary education (11 to 15) and across the whole ability range.

The definition of 'humanities' differed considerably from that of the Humanities Curriculum Project. Humanities to the Integrated Studies Project was understood as any subject, or aspect of a subject, which contributes to the rational or imaginative understanding of the human situation. 'Integration' is understood as the exploration of any large area, theme or problem which (*a*) requires the help of more than one subject discipline for its full understanding; (*b*) is best taught by the concerted action of a team of teachers. Of the possible interpretations of integrated inquiry, the Integrated Studies Project concentrated attention on making possible the study of large and complex human issues. In this respect, it was at one with the Humanities Project; but the selection and treatment of issues differed considerably.

The Integrated Studies Project hoped to achieve integration at three levels: (1) in the mind of a child – the integration of experience; (2) between the forms of knowledge – the organization of several disciplines, or some of their skills and concepts, as appropriate aids to a particular inquiry; (3) in a school – a team of teachers planning, within their given resources, to use areas of knowledge to integrate the child's experience.

The project developed a series of units that form part of a study based on man himself. There were two stages. First-stage units were tried out in the first three years of secondary schools and have since been used in middle schools. They were arranged under three titles: 'Exploration Man', 'Communicating with others', 'Living together'. Some work was done on second-stage units, intended for the fourth and fifth forms, on the themes of 'Man-made-man', 'West Africa' and 'Groups in society'. (Of these, the unit on West Africa will not be published for the Schools Council.) The second-stage units would make impossibly heavy

73

demands on the disadvantaged pupil's reading and comprehension, although teachers might draw on some of the ideas.

The first-stage materials, published by Oxford University Press, contain three units. Unit 1 – *Exploration Man: an Introduction to Integrated Studies* comprises a handbook discussing the philosophy, materials and organization of an integrated curriculum, and introducing working methods and suggestions for a range of activities drawing on familiar objects in the local environment. It is an ideas unit working out of a child's surroundings and experiences. (At the time of the survey it was not intended to publish pupils' materials but subsequent demand led to the publication of six packs of pupils' materials on various themes, with slides and a tape.)*

Unit 2 – 'Communicating with others' and Unit 3 – 'Living together', are packs of sheets and pamphlets, extensively and vividly illustrated and accompanied by an associated tape and sets of full-colour slides.

Five copies of each of the sheets and pamphlets are provided in each section of the units. Thus, it is claimed, one section provides sufficient working material for between thirty and forty children: six sets of a section could provide basic curriculum material for over 120 pupils for one term. A *Teacher's Guide* to Units 2 and 3 contains detailed suggestions for work on the themes of these units.

Some of the themes are of great interest, and no less to the disadvantaged child than to others. It may be helpful to describe one of the units in some detail: Unit 3 – 'Living together', has been chosen because the theme has an obvious appeal. The handbook gives very clear guidance to the teacher on how to plan the inquiry. The aims of Unit 3 are, in general, to encourage an integrated approach to social studies and, in particular:

a   to help pupils achieve a fuller understanding of the structure and functioning of their own society;
b   to encourage tolerance of other cultures, based on insight into different communities;
c   to encourage empathy in the face of human problems;
d   to develop the ability to study societies comparatively;
e   to introduce or reinforce relevant basic study skills.

It was considered by the authors that social activities of central concern to most cultures would include the following: making a home and raising a family; getting

* ATV has produced a series of colour films entitled *Exploration Man* based on themes in Unit 1. (The films were transmitted in autumn 1973.) Prints of the films are available on hire or for sale from the Rank Film Library, PO Box 70, Great West Road, Brentford, Middlesex.

a living and enjoying leisure; social grouping and social control; religious practice and belief. It was largely around this framework of ideas that the material was organized; it was hoped that this offered a structure within which teacher and pupil might work.

The unit falls into two parts. Section A deals with 'Simple societies' – Tristan da Cunha and the Land Dayaks of Borneo – and Section B with a 'Complex society' – Imperial China. The full list of contents is as follows:

SECTION A SIMPLE SOCIETIES

Tristan da Cunha
1. The island
2. Making a living
3. 'Our Tristan houses'
4. Children
5. Growing up
6. Eruption

Land Dayaks of Borneo
1. Land and people
2. Making a living
2a. Work time chart
3. Family and homes
4. Children
5. Ceremony and beliefs
6. Crafts

SECTION B A COMPLEX SOCIETY

Imperial China
1. Land and history
2a. Making a living in North China
2b. Making a living in South China
3. Marriage and parents
4. Children and education
5. Law and order
6. Pottery and painting

7. Stories
8. The dragon symbol
9a. Hangchow in the thirteenth century
9b. Kaifeng in the early twelfth century
10. Technology.

A set of ten slides of art and 'artefacts' is also available to accompany Unit 3B.

The choice of these particular communities was justified as follows: 'It is self-evident that a pupil will have some knowledge of his own society; but this society is highly organized and complex. Basic insights into social organization could be more easily fostered through an approach to communities that are in some way restricted. Pupils can more readily acquire a sense of "wholeness" about a small community than is possible when studying a complex industrialized society.'

Tristan da Cunha was selected as representing a tightly self-contained community which raised the issue of 'culture shock', when the islanders were forced to leave their home and live in Britain, which most of them rejected as a home after a period of two years. The Dayaks of Borneo, an isolated, primitive community, present patterns of social living strikingly relevant to the perennial problems of group living.

It is suggested in the handbook how the following subjects, among others, might contribute: geography, life-style analysis and comparative studies, history and English.

Geography. The geographer could use some of the material for teaching basic skills. Natural phenomena could be identified and classified, e.g. the equatorial rain forest, the volcanic island, etc. The natural environment could be related to the life patterns of the local communities. Pupils could compare and contrast the physical backgrounds, e.g. island/mainland, tropical/temperate, etc.

Life-style analysis and comparative studies. It was hoped that key ideas such as 'role', 'law' or 'culture', which probably could not be taught directly, might be grounded in a number of examples of the unit and possibly other sources.

History. The concern of the historian is for the source and validity of evidence which is available to him. It is possible that the pupil might be made aware of the many sources of evidence which enable an historian to make his assessments, e.g. documents, letters, autobiography, maps, pictures, etc. The historian may also consider change and development in a society. The Tristans suffered a drastic change when forced to evacuate in 1961; they experienced an alternative society and chose to return to their island. But their society could not revert exactly to the status quo. An event outside their control caused them to modify some customs; there were material changes. Children can appreciate the consequences of an event and study the process of change in a very small space and period. It should be easier to isolate some causes of change in their own locality, though hopefully nothing so drastic and dramatic as caused the migration of the Tristans.

English. There will be many opportunities for creative activity – for example, the account of the eruption of the volcano.

Resources available. Most of the material in the Tristan da Cunha section is arranged as leaflets, with numerous photographs, which fold out in a number of different ways; this has the effect of providing unexpected page turnovers but when opened out fully the leaflet can be rather bulky. On the whole, the children seemed to like this arrangement and several teachers commented favourably on the format – though others did not like it. The first piece of evidence is simply information about the island with an interesting hand-drawn map; the second is entitled 'Making a living'; the third describes houses and has on the front a facsimile of a child's hand-written account of his house, and inside an extract from the transcript of the tape-recorded interview with a former chaplain; the fourth deals with children, beginning with the first school on the island in 1906; the fifth is concerned with growing up, the general lack of cultural shock, getting married, setting up home; and the sixth is a graphic account, with newspaper reproductions, of the volcanic eruption of 1961, together with newspaper quotations and transcripts of the tapes of their return in 1963. Also available are tapes of eye-witness accounts of the eruption and points of view about life in Tristan and in England. There is an annotated bibliography of books about Tristan, references to a 'Jackdaw' pack on volcanoes, to the *National Geographic Magazine* and to two films.

Comment on the Integrated Studies Project

It is apparent that this Tristan da Cunha material is of great intrinsic interest to children of the age range 11 to 14 or 15. The tight-knit community has much fascination for most of us and the contrast between the simple life there and the complex industrial technological society which is Britain is given concrete actuality by the journey undertaken by the Tristan islanders. At the level of interest, then, one would expect slow-learning children to share the intense involvement that one could observe with other groups. Although there were difficulties with reading levels, at one inner-city school where the materials were observed boys and girls were overcoming their problems with great alacrity because of the intrinsic motivation provided by this particular unit.

There was, however, a difficulty in providing suitable follow-up activities. Some teachers eventually began to produce supplementary worksheets and structured guidance for the written work which followed discussions. Oral work could very well be arranged with such a wealth of relevant picture material, and the written work could be easily keyed to the more visual elements. For example, Sheet 1 with the map of the island was easy to copy or trace. The same kind of extension material could be provided as that which science teachers have worked out through the Nuffield Science activities, using programming techniques, simple yes/no choices, and again keying most of the activities to the more visual rather than to the verbal. Some of the material on the sheets could be tape-recorded and heard through a junction box, which would greatly extend the number of pupils who could follow the text. The onus, however, remains firmly on the teachers and it is doubtful if the materials in their present form would be immediately useful to most disadvantaged children.

The project was as much concerned with trying out and discussing the methods of integrated studies as with the production of materials. The teacher's handbook and guides provide sensible and practical suggestions about the use of the materials and about the ways in which teachers can extend and develop the studies – for example, by the use of the local environment and by using a wide range of contacts and sources. Features of this approach are, of course, not unknown in schools and in a few schools integration is carried through with enthusiasm and success. Teachers of slow learners, in particular, feel that their pupils are confused by the compartmentalizing of subject matter and that they benefit most from the study of broad themes, particularly if they have reference to the local environment or enlarge their experience through real contacts with the wider world. This project provides a framework of ideas and an approach which would have value for teachers of the disadvantaged. The need is such an important one that we would recommend that the Schools Council should consider setting up a project to explore the need further in relation to academically less successful pupils. In doing so, it would be able to build on and modify the approach of the Integrated Studies Project.

Geography for the Young School Leaver

The Geography for the Young School Leaver Project is based at Avery Hill College of Education, London, and directed by Rex Beddis and Thomas Dalton, with research officers Trevor Higginbottom and Pamela Bowen. It is attempting to provide materials which offer firm guidance but are to a considerable extent open-ended and responsive to local opportunities. The project is developing materials round three themes: 'Man, land and leisure', 'Cities and people' and 'People, place and work'. These are to be published by Nelson during 1974 and 1975.

Four criteria have guided the choice and development of the themes:

1 The work should be concerned with all aspects of pupil development – understanding ideas, acquiring facts, developing skills, engaging attitudes, etc.
2 The themes should be of interest and relevance to the pupils now, but should also be of more than transitory significance.
3 There should be a structure of ideas which focus attention on the concepts of the discipline. These ideas may be initiated by a consideration of the local environment and community. By linkage and analogy these may be extended to more distant parts of Britain and the world.
4 The methods used should encourage full pupil involvement and participation.

78

The project has considered educational needs across the whole ability range.

It is apparent that work in one age or ability grouping in the curriculum has radical implications over a much wider spectrum. For example, to state that something is worth while educationally for the 14- to 16-year-old average to less able pupil might imply that something different is worth while for the more able. This we do not accept. Our schemes, while in technique and methodology designed to assist the less able, in aim and content are designed to meet the needs of 14- to 16-year-olds of all abilities.*

The materials available at the time of writing seemed to be matching the authors' intentions.

Man, Land and Leisure contains five units. These are:

Unit 1. The growing range and increasing significance of leisure.
Unit 2. Leisure provision for local communities
      Part 1 – local study, indoor and outdoor provision of leisure amenities
      Part 2 – an inner-city study: Islington
      Part 3 – open space in a conurbation: Greater London
      Part 4 – planned urban areas: Thamesmead and Basildon New Town
      Part 5 – future town shapes: London and Adelaide.
Unit 3. Leisure in the countryside and national parks
      Part 1 – the National Parks of England and Wales
      Part 2 – the Peak District National Park – conservation and planning.
Unit 4. Leisure and tourism in Britain and Western Europe
      Part 1 – patterns of holidays
      Part 2 – holiday landscapes in Britain (Margate)
      Part 3 – holiday landscapes in Britain (Minehead)
      Part 4 – holiday landscapes in Western Europe, Norway, Central Switzerland, South-east Spain
      Part 5 – holidays and the travel industry
      Part 6 – the seasonal nature of holidays
      Part 7 – tourism as big business.
Unit 5. Leisure – the future.

The materials consist of a teacher's guide to each of the themes, and pupil resources. They are intended to allow for maximum flexibility in use, with the onus for choice of material being left to the teacher. This has the advantage that

* Teacher's guide to *Man, Land and Leisure*.

the materials are not limited to any particular organizational framework. At the time of the survey only trial materials were available, but even at this stage materials were of a high quality. To take an example: Unit 1 – The growing range and increasing significance of leisure. The resources provided were photo-sheets, discussion sheets and a filmstrip. The discussion sheets employed a variety of formats, most of which were successful, and the diagrams were very clear. The content of some of the newspaper articles reproduced would still present difficulties for the children with lowest attainments. Under the heading 'Leisure time – where can you spend it?' four admirable black-and-white photo-graphs showed the interior of some Welsh caves, a jazz and blues festival, a swimming pool and yachting on the Norfolk Broads. A further sheet showed a group watching a football match, with two of the boys in close-up enjoying an intimate conversation; another picture showed a boy sitting in a tree reading, with a caption 'On your own'; other scenes showed a family group on the beach and a group of teenagers sitting on the steps at Trafalgar Square. The worksheets would be usable by most children, even those with minimal reading attainment. Some of the discussion sheets, such as 'What are you doing tonight?' were in cartoon-strip form with the conversation in balloons and this format seemed highly successful.

Much of this work seems to regard geography in a much wider sense than the stereotype of that subject would suggest. Schools Council Working Paper No. 11, *Society and the Young School Leaver: a Humanities Programme in Preparation for the Raising of the School Leaving Age* (HMSO, 1967), speaks of identifying 'centres of interest' or 'areas of inquiry' and by doing so finding it possible to teach not less but more of the individual disciplines, because they are being learned not for their own sake but to make clear the answer to part of a larger problem. The project sees the role of geography, whether as a separate subject or integrated with other subject disciplines, as that of answering real questions which the pupils can be interested in. The geographer, having an interest in man's response to his environment – whether that environment be physical or man-made – in location, spatial patterns and processes, is seen as being equipped to make a distinctive contribution to such contemporary themes as leisure, urbanization and work.

Obviously the project favours some form of team-teaching or other collabora-tion between specialists and in one of the schools involved in the project, specialists in English, geography, history and religious education had been presenting a course entitled humanities. One teacher in a trial school concerned with presenting Geography for the Young School Leaver to fourth-year leavers had grave initial doubts about its application to disadvantaged pupils – the vocabulary and concepts appeared to be well above the capabilities of his group, many of whom were virtually illiterate. Yet most of the work was successful and this seemed to be due to:

a   the variety and the presentation of the material supplied;
b   the fact that there was a considerable local element in the work;
c   the liaison between the project team and the local schools involved;
d   the variety of equipment and other resources available in this school of two thousand pupils.

Some of the work described raised issues of urban land-use conflict, and certainly represents a considerable extension of the traditional subject matter of geography.

> One lesson which sticks out in my mind is that based on 'Battling for a play space' (LE/2/E/3). The class entered the room to find LE/2/E/3 on their desks and the good readers helped the less able through the passage. The pupils were then told that they were a deputation which had come to attempt to discuss the situation outlined in the passage. I explained that I would play the part of an official and that I would answer any points that they wished to raise. I then left the room and gave the class a few minutes to discuss their approach. When I entered the room I adopted a belligerent attitude and before long the deputation really got into the role they were playing and we had what was probably the best discussion session of the year.
>
> In the second part of the lesson the class was divided into two groups. Some of the pupils wrote a short play while others only wanted to write an account of the main points put forward in the previous discussion. Three remedial children and two of the more able pupils went into another room and made a recording of a discussion they had among themselves along the lines of the earlier part of the lesson. This small group was completely uninhibited and produced a piece of work of which they were very proud.*

This teacher overcame the difficulties presented by a mixed-ability class by allowing the pupils to work in small groups; by paraphrasing difficult reading matter; by much discussion, including interpretation of photographs. 'For those children who had the greatest difficulty with reading and writing, a tape-recorder was most useful and it gave them some self-confidence for they were able to produce results as good as anyone else's in the class.'

This degree of flexibility was not shown by all the teachers who were involved, and there is no doubt that some of the reading matter is pitched at too high a

* Gwyn Lewis, 'Geography for the Young School Leaver with less able pupils', *The Project in Schools* (Geography for the Young School Leaver Project, 1972).

level; this is more obvious in the 'Cities and people' theme materials. For example, worksheets on inner-city redevelopment deal with the Hyde Park ('streets in the sky') housing complex in Sheffield. Some very difficult vocabulary is included and the task of completing a census-style environment survey seemed very demanding, with cross-references required between tapes and several visual sources, as well as a lengthy text.

The general enthusiasm of teachers at one of the regional meetings we were able to attend was, therefore, very encouraging. Among the features selected for special mention were:

a the variety and ingenuity of the transparencies and overlays provided for the overhead projector – adaptable for use without the hardware;
b the quality and wit of the set of slides giving an historical perspective on urban congestion;
c the quality of four photosheets provided on cities and homes;
d the quality of the taped interviews with local people;
e the aerial photography which was much appreciated.

Obviously, the theme 'Cities and people' has a special application to many of the disadvantaged pupils we are concerned with. A considerable proportion live in urban areas and it is sensible to study the environment in which one lives. Pupils at the secondary stage of their education might be enabled to see their home circumstances in a different light, if they could be made aware that certain characteristics of cities appear to be universal: inadequate provision of houses; outward sprawl; competition for land at the centre, resulting in high-rise development.

To help disadvantaged pupils place themselves in time and space is, indeed, a laudable educational objective because they, more than anyone, tend to be rooted in the immediate and the local. So the project hopes to encourage *attitudes* – an awareness of the common human problems that exist in most cities of the world as a result of inadequate supply of housing or of sub-standard conditions, and an appreciation of the conflicting priorities of various age groups for amenities in a given urban area; and *skills* – such as the use of an atlas, ability to interpret simple statistics, elementary map construction, and (yet again) discussion.

One technique proposed asks about a person's mental map of his environment – which usually differs from reality and reflects his age, degree of mobility and, possibly, social group. Detailed suggestions are made in the *Teacher's Guide*. No information about the effectiveness of this exercise was available at the time of writing, but it would seem to be relevant to our population.

82

Conclusions

The aims of this project and the methods of learning and inquiry which it proposes seem as appropriate to slow-learning and disadvantaged children as to more able pupils. Less successful pupils should be helped by the range and variety of materials – pictures, slides, aerial photographs and maps, and by the emphasis on activity and inquiry. The reading required is not too demanding and the information could easily be communicated in other ways.

It is our impression that involvement in the activities proposed by the project could be undertaken particularly in groups of mixed ability by some of the slowest children and that teachers of children in special schools for the ESN might give consideration to some aspects of this project. Teachers of less successful children will often have had experience of initiating local studies and inquiries into leisure and will be ready to benefit from the suggestions and guidance of the project. The various materials available should provide an extra stimulus to pupils.

North West Regional Curriculum Development Project

Social education

Materials from this project (published by Macmillan Education) include a one-year course entitled 'Vocation', and a two-year course in social education divided into six topics: 'Freedom and responsibility', 'Consumer education', 'Conservation', 'Marriage and home-making', 'Towards tomorrow' and 'The British', each topic designed to last a term. There is much emphasis on personal responsibility.

All the material has been tried in schools with groups of up to 120 pupils in rural and urban conditions; it has been used primarily with less able pupils aged about 11 to 16, but has also been the basis of courses preparing for Mode III CSE.

The one-year course entitled 'Vocation' tries to help young people to see themselves in relation to the community and to help them come to terms with their future role in society, with particular reference to work.

Although the materials could be described as traditional in content, the presentation is varied, incorporating tapes, filmstrips, information sheets and pads of expendable worksheets. The teaching techniques which are favoured include discussion; visits; the design, administration and completion of questionnaires; interviews; the use of industrial and commercial firms' promotional material for display purposes; the use of newspapers for background information; and frequent recourse to outside speakers.

The pupils are encouraged initially to examine their own strengths and weaknesses, aptitudes and abilities, likes and dislikes. They are then encouraged to examine the resources of the district and to determine their own potential within the opportunities available. The unit dealing with 'The world of work' provides for visits to places of work, visits from the personnel or training officers, from a trade-union representative, and for the showing of a variety of films. Particularly interesting is the use of pupils' own voices in the preparation of the tapes (at least they sound entirely authentic). The kind of discussion which tends to emerge again shows some degree of consensus with the Moral Education Curriculum Project materials. For example, 'Vocation' Unit 21 has a work 'situation' entitled 'Spoiling a job'. This deals, in broad Lancashire accents, with a situation where two young mechanics have skimped a job, with the result that a car has been taken away with the job uncompleted and the brakes unsafe. In another, two girls discuss a situation where a third girl has been seen to steal goods in a chain-store. One girl favours reporting the thief, even though the latter is a close friend of hers; the other vigorously opposes this course of action on the grounds that one cannot 'split'. In a third situation, two young men discuss the practice known as 'working a foreigner' – in which the man uses materials and vehicles belonging to his firm to complete jobs of his own during the firm's time. Tom regards this practice as reprehensible but Bert can see no harm in it – the only alternative to working hard, finishing soon and using the time for his own advantage, seems to be to work slowly and fill in the time. A fourth work situation deals with clocking-in for a friend. Sue earnestly entreats Martha to clock in for her although she cannot go to work because she feels poorly, and seems to have persuaded Martha against her better judgement to perform this service for her. These are interesting situations and the tapes bring them alive; they are linked to filmstrips, which have appropriate frames linked to the tape by means of a signal button. Using this arrangement, there seems no reason why pupils should not be able to work independently. Particularly pleasing is the large-scale use of disposable worksheets, which are provided in tear-off pads.

The section on 'Self-assessment' is very well-developed, beginning with simple self-completed questionnaires which, in their simplest form, provide a blank sheet with name and personal qualities, moving through 'In my opinion, my form teacher/tutor thinks I am', 'My parents think', 'My best friend thinks', 'I think I am really', to a self-assessment questionnaire asking them to rate themselves on a three-point scale on such items as 'Are you sociable?', 'Are you a leader?', 'Are you completely honest?', 'Are you conscientious?', 'Are you reliable?', 'Are you courteous and polite?', 'Are you respectful of authority?' The process is terminated by a graph showing 'My self-assessment in comparison with other people's assessment of me.' These questionnaires are linked to the tapes, one of the most interesting of which has discussions by various people, and a boy and girl pupil. This really does have the effect of giving a many-sided portrait and might well cause an individual to reassess himself or herself. To aid this process further, a series of profile cards is provided with a picture of actual boys and girls and a summary of personal qualities under headings: name, age, home background, school, school record, likes, dislikes.

Reports from schools which helped to develop the materials were enthusiastic. This is very practical material, intended to be immediately useful in the class-room. The tapes and slides on interview technique may be very helpful to 'candidates' who present themselves as badly as some of those depicted; they do not focus on broad issues, such as the possible consequences if both candidates do well but one is, nevertheless, rejected. The self-assessment and interview techniques have long been a stock-in-trade of youth employment officers; these materials are good of their kind, however – the illustrations, for example, are highly contemporary and this matters enormously with disadvantaged pupils.

The two-year social education course includes many controversial issues, but the treatment is far removed from the Humanities Curriculum Project. There is little discussion of the teacher's role; instead, a plethora of pupils' materials is provided and their utilization left in the hands of the teachers. The materials are pitched near the right level and they include expendable worksheets, information sheets (with unfussy photographs), filmstrips and pre-recorded tapes, which greatly help to extend the potential audience. One must feel well disposed towards this material because it so clearly reflects the teacher's view of what is required.

The situations created on the tapes and in the filmstrips deal with real issues: freedom at home, at school and in the community; responsibilities at home; points of conflict (and some of these are the very same as Peter McPhail identified for his Moral Education Curriculum Project).

The following extract is from one of the information sheets:

Carol: It's not fair. Listen, I want to go. I'm sorry, dad, but I don't want to be following you around Eastbourne. If he can go on holiday with his friends that means I'm going to be left with you and I'm going to be lonely.

Dad: So you're willing to make your mother's holiday a misery. She slaves her heart out fifty weeks a year . . .

Carol: Well, what's so different about me and Pete? Why can Pete go and not me?

Dad: Because you're a girl.

Peter: What difference does that make?

Dad: Because I don't want her coming back pregnant.

Summary

The projects discussed in this chapter provide a variety of approaches to the humanities. Several of them have been used successfully with disadvantaged children including slow learners and children with literacy problems. For the teacher keen to widen the curriculum experiences of less successful pupils, the exploration of methods of teaching and organization which these projects support would be as important as the materials produced by the projects although, as we recommend in our conclusions in Chapter II, we see scope for a development project which, by producing additional materials, would assist teachers working with children who are the lowest in ability and attainment. Since these are children who often have most need of help in order to understand themselves and the society in which they live, the humanities is an area of the curriculum which we should ensure is brought within their grasp.

VI. Moral and religious education

Moral Education Curriculum Project

The Moral Education Curriculum Project (1967-72) was based at the Department of Educational Studies, University of Oxford, under the directorship of Peter McPhail. The teaching materials are published by Longman.

The discussion of everyday moral issues and behaviour in social situations is something needed by all pupils but particularly by slow-learning and disadvantaged children. Apart from provision for this in religious education, such discussion often occurs incidentally in the course of other activities – sometimes a sympathetic teacher of needlework, housecraft, woodwork, history or English finds topics being referred to which are obviously of real concern to adolescents. The teacher who has a good relationship with pupils and has the experience and maturity (not necessarily a question of age) is able to nourish and facilitate talk about matters which help the development of social attitudes and competence.

The ideas and materials of the Moral Education Curriculum Project appeared to provide a useful contribution to this field. They also seemed suited to disadvantaged children, for the following reasons:

a   the topics included in the materials were familiar and simple situations within the experience of disadvantaged children;
b   the materials demanded little or no reading ability;
c   a variety of pupil activity was envisaged – dramatization and role-play, painting and other forms of creative work, as well as discussion and free writing.

Since there was little information about the use of the materials with disadvantaged children, we arranged a small trial of the materials in a number of secondary and special schools. This is reported later, but we should first consider some of the background ideas of Peter McPhail, the Project Director.

The Moral Education Curriculum Project regards social skills as having much in common with motor skills (such as cycling, skating, driving a car, playing the piano, typing, performing industrial tasks, playing tennis and other games) in that they can be learnt. If we accept this, it is possible to take a more optimistic view of the outcome of training in certain social skills.

McPhail hypothesized that adolescence is a period during which the number of 'social experiments' made by an individual reaches a peak and then falls again. He defined a 'social experiment' as 'any situation when an individual exhibits a trial attitude or takes a trial course of action which calls forth and effects a reaction from any other individual or group of individuals, whether the attitude is adopted or action taken with a view to testing reaction, or with no conscious aim.'

The 'social experiment' in McPhail's view (supported by the evidence of a large-scale inquiry) is a learning situation. A development of the argument is that the most fundamental kind of human learning is experimental or trial-and-error learning (even when this involves imitation). 'The contention is that a sense of identity only follows the ability to predict the effects of one's actions and to modify one's environment.' The adolescent asks 'Who am I?' and this leads to other questions: 'What can I cope with?', 'Is my self-concept accepted by others?', 'Is my social approach effective in terms of establishing the relationship I want?'

The Moral Education Curriculum Project rested upon sound theoretical foundations and McPhail's own theoretical expositions are admirably concise. But the project has adopted a very pragmatic approach. The project's working answer to the question *What is moral education?* was that *all education which helped a child to adopt a considerate style of life, to have respect for others' feelings and interests as well as his own, was moral education.* Doctrine was confined to the assertion that 'a world in which people are treated with consideration for their feelings and interests is preferable to one in which this is not the case – a piece of assertiveness which seemed unlikely to cut us off from the followers of any of the great religions or from agnostic or atheistic humanists.'*

Materials

Varied materials have been published under the series title *Lifeline*. They include suggestions for the use of discussion, role-play, creative writing and art. The programme is designed to lead pupils from familiar and simple situations towards more complex and less immediately recognizable problems. The first group of materials is called 'In Other People's Shoes'. Three sets of cards entitled *Sensitivity*, *Consequences* and *Points of View* introduce incidents in everyday surroundings. For example, pupils are given the girl's and boy's point of view on the question of a strenuous canoeing holiday and are asked what they would do in a similar situation. There is also a teacher's guide with the first group. The second group called 'Proving the Rule?', comprises five short books: *Rules and In-*

* P. McPhail, 'The Moral Education Curriculum Project' in *Let's Teach Them Right* ed. C. Macy and H. J. Blackham (Pemberton Books, 1969).

dividuals, *What do you Expect?*, *Who do you think I am?*, *In whose Interest?* and *Why should I?* It deals primarily with the behaviour of small groups, again in familiar settings. The third group, 'What Would You Have Done?', has six booklets: *Birth Day, South Africa 1904*; *Solitary Confinement, Lincolnshire 1917*; *Arrest! Amsterdam 1944*; *Street Scene, Los Angeles 1965*; *Hard Luck Story, South Vietnam 1966*; and *Gail in Hospital, London 1969*. It contains topic material based on incidents from the recent past, such as the arrest of the Frank family in Nazi Europe, the 1965 Los Angeles riots, etc. (There are also sets of slides to accompany this group of booklets.)* Other publications include *Our School*, a handbook for teachers and students on the practice of democracy by secondary-school pupils, and *Moral Education in the Secondary School*, a book introducing the programme, outlining the rationale and relating the materials.

The importance of role-play over mere discussion is emphasized. Forty-six stimulus situations are provided, each illustrated with a humorous drawing. In addition, twenty-four work cards are provided for the pupils to use as individuals or in groups, selectively or at random.

The *Teacher's Guide* for 'In Other People's Shoes' provides a list of the situations on which discussion and role-playing could be based. Some examples are:

1. You are very attracted to a girl/boy but she/he ignores you.
2. A boy or girl of your own age with whom you are friendly appears to be very upset for some reason unknown to you.
3. You suggest to a friend that you both go on the 'big wheel' at a fair but your friend seems reluctant.
7. The person in the next desk to you sniffs continually.
8. Your parents brag about you to their friends in your presence.
12. Your father is critical of your hair and of your clothes.
14. Your mother herself adopts teenage fashions.
17. An adult is critical of your parents in their absence.
31. You lend a coat to your cousin. When the coat is returned there is a cigarette burn in the lapel.
38. A boy in your form thinks that it is amusing to let down your bicycle tyres.

Suggestions for classroom use:

(a) Read out or write on the board 'a situation' for consideration.
(b) Ask the members of the form to write down on a piece of paper what they would do in this situation. (The backward can be asked to think what they would do.)

* Slides are available from Slide Centre Ltd, Portman House, 17 Brodrick Road, London SW17 7DZ.

(c) Ask for suggested courses of action or collect the papers and choose one to start with.

(d) Invite a group of children who have made a similar response to role-play the situation, the response to it and what they think would happen subsequently. (If they are initially reluctant, invite volunteers or ask them to argue in support of their response and encourage a discussion.)

(e) Initiate form criticism of the response and any other aspects of the role-play.

(f) Continue by inviting the role-play and/or discussion of further responses suggested by the children only as long as interest is strongly maintained.

(g) Some summing up by the form and the teacher is in order, but an obvious and emphatic commitment to one response by the teacher during the early stages of this work is not to be encouraged. It is better to discuss the pros and cons of different courses of action and leave the children to make a final judgement.

A technique for assessing the pupils' responses is provided. This is best illustrated by reproducing an example:

1. You are very attracted to a girl/boy but she/he ignores you. What do you do?

Classification	Response
Passive	Shrug your shoulders and forget it
Passive–emotional	Feel angry but don't know what to do
Dependent–adult	Talk to an adult about the situation
Dependent–peer	Talk to a friend about what you should do
Aggressive	Become very critical of that girl or boy
Very aggressive	Make life as difficult for that girl/boy as you can
Avoidance	Avoid seeing the person concerned
Experimental–crude	Try to make the person concerned take notice of you, for example, by showing off
Experimental–sophisticated	Attempt to make yourself attractive by being agreeable
Mature–conventional	Persist for a time before, if necessary, finding another girl/boy friend
Mature–imaginative	Find out what she/he is interested in and approach her/him through the interest, while recognizing that you are not the answer to everyone's prayer!

It is certainly not intended that the teacher should pick out a 'good' response for the pupils and give it to them under the impression that he has done what is

90

necessary to educate them morally! The purpose of using the system of classification is fourfold:

a   to help the teacher to recognize the possibilities in a given situation;
b   to help the teacher to recognize the adolescent's difficulties so as to be in a better position to assist him;
c   to provide a list of responses which the teacher can use as further subjects for discussion, role-play, etc., in a form where the courses of action suggested have been limited;
d   to enable boys and girls to understand their own and others' responses better as a preliminary to evaluating them in moral terms and ultimately improving their performances.

A small-scale trial of Moral Education Curriculum Project materials with slow learners

Since there was only a little information about the use of the project with disadvantaged children it was decided, with the ready agreement of Peter McPhail, to arrange for a number of schools in the West Midlands to use the materials so that the reaction of teachers and pupils could be gauged.

Four comprehensive schools took part, in two cases using the materials with a second-year remedial group, in two cases with fourth-year leavers not doing examinations. In one of the schools, a second teacher used the materials with average pupils. In two special schools for ESN children, the materials were used with third- and fourth-year pupils in whom the usual variety of handicaps in ability, communication and difficult behaviour were represented.

The teachers taking part in the trial spent a day being briefed by Peter McPhail on the aims of the project and the nature and use of the materials. After two terms of using them, the teachers again met to report their experiences. (The report from one comprehensive school is reproduced as Appendix A.) The materials made available were *Sensitivity*, *Consequences* and *Points of View*, the first set being the most used.

Such a limited trial can do no more than give some tentative impressions of the suitability of the materials and indicate if there are any difficulties.

Suitability of the materials

In general, the teachers found the materials very suitable for disadvantaged children. The fact that reading was not essential and that the situations to be discussed or acted could be presented orally was one obvious advantage. The fact that the topics were everyday ones, familiar to pupils' experience, meant that there was no difficulty in basic understanding of the problem. Situations such as having your bicycle tyres let down, conflict with parents or grandparents about fashions, hair-styles, pop music on the radio or difficulties in friendships are common enough. What many slow-learning and disadvantaged children may not have done is to think further about such incidents, seeing them from the other person's point of view or imagining the consequences. While the level of discussion may not be high, it is surely a step in the right direction if, as happened in one of the special school groups, children become more aware that parents at home have a point of view which has to be taken into account or that some apparently trivial behaviour like throwing stones at a bottle on a beach may have serious consequences. It is common to find that slow learners do not think of the consequences of their actions nor the reaction of other people to their behaviour.

The teachers reported, as one might expect, that some topics had been found less appropriate for pupils of certain age groups and from certain backgrounds. Thus one school found that the lowest stream of 13- to 14-year-olds had not reached the stage of being really interested in situations involving the opposite sex though this had changed by the age of 15. These 13- to 14-year-olds were more interested in such questions as whether it was right to run errands for their mother, than whether boys and girls should share the same interests and activities on holidays. It was felt that many more situations involving parents and children and even relations with prefects in school and neighbours in the classroom might be advantageous. These comments probably reflect a tendency for some groups of disadvantaged children to be somewhat immature emotionally and in their interests – a point which is, of course, significant in selecting topics in many curriculum areas. On the other hand, with a group of ESN leavers, it was situations such as another boy interfering with an existing boy–girl relationship which aroused most interest. The teacher reported that even the most silent of her children had been roused to speak. She instanced an extremely anti-social girl who had been won over by the material because the situations were those she knew about and she could contribute. Another school found that some questions were scarcely relevant to the children's background – thus, the situation of a boy and girl discussing household jobs could be unreal because many of the boys were not expected to and did not intend to do anything in the house.

In general, our impression that the *Lifeline* materials were well suited to disadvantaged children, both in the topics and in the concrete situations presented, seemed to be confirmed by the experience of teachers using them. One teacher made the point that much of the material was, in fact, similar to work she had been accustomed to undertake with slow learners but having the material and appreciating the underlying ideas of the project had provided a very useful framework.

92

As frequently happens, several teachers commented on the reluctance of pupils to give their views but others reported that groups had spoken out freely from the beginning. One teacher found that a more able group was more ready to discuss than to engage in role-play or dramatization. In one of the ESN schools, however, it was dramatization which set the group alight – the children were markedly limited in the ability to express themselves and several had speech defects. Dramatizing topics made the situation concrete, helped comprehension and certainly provoked some normally silent ones to contribute verbally.

The teachers agreed that it was difficult to avoid leading the discussion too much and also difficult to decide whether pupils were actually giving their own opinions or giving what they thought the teacher might want. It was felt that time was needed to develop the habit of contributing to an oral discussion – and obviously the schools varied in the extent to which discussion had been practised before, formally as well as informally. One quite verbal group had produced a fine crop of short stories; another had gone on to make a play and this work continued for four sessions.

In the final teachers' discussion, the point was made that the use of either discussion or role-play might depend on what suited the teacher better; some teachers do not themselves feel comfortable at taking part in a role-playing session. There is no doubt that role-play (dramatization or socio-drama) has a releasing effect on the response of pupils. If they are not familiar with improvised drama, embarrassment may lead to some foolishness at first. The gradual initiation into the use of socio-drama suggested by the Social Education Project (see page 60) is worth consideration. It is significant that Peter McPhail emphasizes role-play in moral education on the grounds that more is learnt from acting than from just talking. The truth of this is certainly obvious with very slow-learning children. One may talk at length about situations they may meet in the family and in working life after they leave school but the lesson is much more likely to be learnt by dramatizing the social situation.

In the short time available for the trial it was not to be expected that dramatic changes in attitude or ways of thinking about problems would be observed. However, whereas at the beginning disadvantaged children tended to see things in black and white and were not likely to see a compromise solution, there were indications, as the work went on, of a more reasoned approach to questions. One might reasonably expect that using *Lifeline* over a longer period would have a positive effect on pupils' moral and social awareness. One would hope that sensitivity to other people's points of view and the experience of role-play would help adjustment and social behaviour in practice.

Summary

These materials are well worth the attention of teachers of slow learners and disadvantaged children for the following reasons:

1   They deal with an area of education acknowledged to be important but where there is, for a variety of reasons, uncertainty about the methods to be employed. Probably not enough effort is made to help pupils think about moral issues and social behaviour.
2   These materials are practical and down-to-earth and seem readily accepted by teachers and pupils.
3   They are very suitable for use with less successful pupils, with no particular modifications being needed, though teachers will obviously wish to select topics and the approach according to the interests and emotional maturity of pupils.
4   The use of the materials has several side-benefits such as providing practice in oral language and expression as well as facilitating various forms of creative work.

Religious Education in Secondary Schools

This project was established in 1969, at the Religious Studies Department of the University of Lancaster under the direction of Professor Ninian Smart. It finished in 1973. The project aimed to evolve materials which could be used by both teachers and pupils in a satisfying programme of secondary-school religious education, taking into account the special needs and emphases of the different types of school as well as the presence of non-Christian populations in this country.

The project set up work-groups in a number of regions and provided preliminary guidance for teams of teachers to produce teaching materials which, it was hoped, would be applicable over a wide range of ability.

A substantial body of work has resulted, and publication of the materials by Hart-Davis Educational will begin in 1975. Despite efforts made by the project team and some local groups of teachers to produce materials for less-able children, much of the trial material we saw was couched in terms and at a level of concept which would make it difficult to use with such children. Nevertheless, the treatment of some themes is extremely useful and obviously could be adapted by a teacher. Some units, for example, recommend audio-visual support, and with filmstrips or slides much of the material could be used across the whole ability range. Themes such as 'Freedom and responsibility' are included and it is sug-

94

gested that this would be suitable for the 13- to 14-year-old age range and with Mode III CSE pupils.

Details of the 'Freedom and responsibility' theme

The aims of this theme were:

1 to encourage the pupil to explore the concept of individual freedom and to relate it to ideas of the individual's responsibility to society;
2 to foster an understanding of some of the sacrifices which others have had to make in order to defend their freedom;
3 to enable the pupil to learn something about the Christian ideal of freedom under God.

The objectives were:

1 to introduce the pupil to the challenge offered by those who stand up for freedom in difficult situations;
2 to help the pupil to explore the ideal of freedom through poetry, music and drama;
3 to provide an opportunity for a mature understanding of some of the many forms of physical, mental and spiritual captivity.

The content includes:

Lesson 1 – Introduction – 'I have a Dream' – filmstrip and tape-recording.
Lesson 2 – Captivity – physical, mental and spiritual.
Lesson 3 – What it means to be free – group discussion.
Lesson 4 – Freedom in poetry and song – recordings, readings, creative writing.
Lesson 5 – How free are you? – Discussion based on a series of coloured slides.
Lesson 6 – Pressures through advertising – questionnaire followed by discussion with further series of coloured slides.
Lesson 7 – Review of service on freedom or a session of role-playing.

Lesson 1 opens with the suggestion – 'Show the filmstrip if there is time. A short discussion on one or two points in it could be useful. It is advisable for the teacher to play the tape and look at the script before showing it to the class so that the discussion afterwards is not unprepared.'

One theme is 'Islam and the Muslim way of life'. The age range is 11 to 12 years, but the ability grouping is average and above average. However, the theme clearly has great interest to those working in areas where multiracial populations exist. One of the sections is entitled 'Meeting point' and discusses Muslims in Britain. Another is called 'Why wear that?'; another 'A visit to the mosque' and another 'Friday at the mosque'. This material is extremely well developed and again includes a filmstrip which can be used to illustrate parts of the mosque, explanatory notes and a conversation between a Muslim child and an English child. There is a tape which is the second of two on Islam prepared by Radio Durham as part of a series on world religions. The main items on the tape are: 'Calls to worship', 'Christian and Muslim', 'Deciding the time of the Friday prayer', 'Inside the mosque', 'Prayer beads', 'Decoration of the mosque', etc., 'The names of Allah'.

Another theme is 'How others see life'. This is intended for 13- to 14-year-olds of all abilities. It again deals with different religions. Its aims are:

1 to teach some facts about some of the living religions of the world, particularly the faith of immigrant groups;
2 to foster a better understanding of the spiritual value of these faiths;
3 to break down the prejudices against immigrants which exist in parts of this country, and to act as a prophylactic against the growth of further prejudice.

The material on this theme has a week-by-week scheme dealing with the Hindu, the Buddhist, the Muslim, the Sikh, the Jew, the Christian.

These are only a few examples from a considerable amount of material but it is perhaps enough to indicate the lines along which development is proceeding in this delicate area of the curriculum. Though, as indicated, much of the material as it exists at present would be unusable with disadvantaged children, it is excellent as a source of ideas, and the audio-visual material provides plenty of opportunities for the teacher who prefers to create his or her own lesson but welcomes enlightened guidance.

VII. Science

Nuffield Junior Science

One of the earliest of the science projects was the Nuffield Junior Science Project (1964–66) .This set a pattern of evaluating teaching materials in a number of pilot areas and of involving LEAs and colleges of education through the teachers' centres which were set up from 1965 onwards. The Nuffield Junior Science Project produced materials consisting of two teachers' guides; source books of information and ideas, *Apparatus* and *Animals and Plants*; and teachers' background booklets, *Autumn into Winter, Science and History* and *Mammals in Classrooms*. These are all published by Collins.

Teacher's Guide 1 opens with a quotation from John Dewey: 'Children are people. They grow into tomorrow only as they live today.' After this it is no surprise to find that the approach relies heavily upon first-hand sensory experience: 'it is vital that the child should *handle* materials, as well as hear, smell and taste them too, if that is practicable. The value of such experience cannot be overestimated and there can be no substitute for it.' Films, books, radio, television and verbal explanations can extend the quality of understanding but cannot replace it: 'We believe that the child thinks as a result of the vast experience which is constantly flowing in through his senses . . . an 11-year-old in a secondary school had to place on his tongue a tiny grain of salt he had recovered from a solution, even though he knew perfectly well that nothing but salt had been dissolved in the water.'

This philosophy was given classroom reality through the project authors' belief that children's practical problem-solving is essentially a scientific way of working, so the task in school is not one of teaching science to children, but rather of utilizing the children's own way of working – which may have scientific characteristics – as a potent educational tool. This could be achieved by giving careful attention to the children's own questions – these often seemed to be most significant and to result most often in careful investigations. Science, which is essentially a practical study of the environment, can go some way towards meeting a restricted and egocentric view of the environment which shows itself in a readiness to make inquiries for a practical purpose, but a far smaller interest in asking questions for their own sake. Slow-learning children do not seem to ask questions readily and the ones they do ask are those to which it is possible to find

97

immediate answers rather than long-term answers. They do not often venture into the realm of abstract thought and they seek answers at a superficial level. To understand they need even more concrete experience than others. For example, Rosemary, aged 16, went on for a whole afternoon filling three boxes of different dimensions with water before she was satisfied that they held the same amount. At the end of the session, she could not see that bottles of different shapes might have the same capacity and had to go through the same concrete experiences with them. The authors warned, therefore, that when we say a child cannot understand, we frequently mean that he has not had sufficient experience of the right kind *to be able* to understand.

'Carol was exactly the same age as Rosemary and had the same IQ. She not only understood that the three boxes had the same capacity but could also explain how this was possible. For months, she had been doing a weekend job of washing up in a hotel and handled many glasses, mugs, flagons, etc., having similar capacities but different shapes. This extensive experience may well have helped her to understand.' The authors suggest that the value of scientific inquiry to slow-learning children is threefold:

(a) It helps them to learn about their surroundings in a way which is natural and acceptable to them, i.e. by practical exploration relying heavily on sensory experience.

(b) It is extremely satisfying and valuable for them to feel personally involved and to meet with success in a world which so often appears to reject them and in which they fail. For this to happen, the problem being tackled must be their own and at their own level.

(c) Involvement and discovery – however limited their scope – help the child to communicate. The teachers who have worked with us all agree that this is of major effect. So often, the slow learner has very little that he wants to say or is able to say and as a result he is frequently a withdrawn and uncommunicative person. We have found that when a child personally and practically makes a discovery, this usually gives him something he *wants* to say and makes him seek a way.

Integrated activities

Teacher's Guide 1 contains innumerable examples of ways in which there can be interaction between different classroom activities. For example, there is a painting by older juniors based on careful observation of insects; a clay model of a snail; models of insects made with paper and wire; written work based on the oil-fired boiler system in the school. 'I went to the boiler house and I saw a switchboard and I saw a fire and the fire is hot and I saw a bike and there was a box in the boiler house.' Both the teachers' guides are full of information and actual illustrations of lessons in progress. There are suggestions for further work. For example, 'Scrap materials left on waste ground' might produce sessions as follows:

Metals – corrosion and its prevention. Properties of different metals.
Tubular steel from bicycle frames, prams, etc. – strength of tubes compared with rods or strips of similar weight.
Wheels from cycles and prams – cog wheels, chains and belts. Leading to study of machines, gear ratios, friction.
Springs – elasticity of materials. Breaking strains.
Tyres – rubber as a tough, flexible material which will withstand wear, piercing, flexing, warmth, etc. Tread pattern and grip.
Metal cans – reflection in plane and curved surfaces.
Bottles – which tip easily? Balance and centre of gravity. Refraction and reflection of light.
Wood – pattern of the grain and how made. Hardness of different woods. Rotting and timber preservation. Cracking.

Under each of these headings there is a short note on method of procedure and a list of references. Such work has a special relevance to the inner-city environment since it stresses opportunities instead of over-emphasizing problems.

The authors believed that science in the first two years should be related to past and present experience and to the needs and interests of the pupils. The learning is intended to be entirely child-centred. A theme such as plastics or heat may be sufficient to act as a starting point; it is suggested that before long the children will themselves impose some kind of system. For example, starting from the topic 'heat', within three weeks two boys were asking for sheet aluminium to construct a solar mirror. The rest of the class was busily engaged in investigations which were not traditional ones but which required many of the techniques the teacher had been anxious about. 'Experience has shown that over a period of time, children following a completely free-ranging study will involve themselves in all the traditional areas of science and will learn to use all the traditional tools and techniques.' While recognizing that some teachers will find this situation somewhat stressful, the project nevertheless recommended most strongly that the teacher should allow the detailed patterns of investigation to grow out of the children's own interests.

Teacher's Guide 2 contains classroom examples. These include, for the age range 9–13 (boys and girls), the examples given in the table below.

Apparatus, a source book of information and ideas, is a collection of photographs and descriptions of apparatus designed and made by children and teachers. It is intended for reference, to give support to teachers who are making a start, and as an example and stimulus for the creation of further apparatus. There are sections on elementary electricity, biological apparatus, light, machines, air, sound and heat, water, weather and soil studies, and on furniture and equipment, with an appendix on the storing of apparatus and equipment.

Title	Age	Ability	Type of area
Central heating	9–10	full range	urban
Leaves	9–10	upper of two streams	urban
A nature trail	9–10	full range	urban
A school playing field	9–10	full range	urban
Sound II	9–10	full range	urban
Bricks and glass	9–11	full range	urban
A weather saying, birds, and a woollen mill	9–11	full range	rural
Urban wasteland	9–11	full range	urban
A woodland visit	9–11	mainly below average	urban
Angling	10–11	average and below	urban
A farm visit	10–11	full range	suburban
Birds and other things on the playing fields	10–11	full range	urban
Lead smelting	11–12	full range	rural
Felling a tree	12–13	third of four streams	suburban

Animals and Plants is another reference work giving precise and accurate information about a variety of living creatures and including detailed advice on how to house and care for those which can be kept in the classroom, as well as suggesting ways in which they might be used there. The animals are grouped under Mammals, Amphibia and Reptiles, Aquatic, Insects, etc. The part on plants contains the following sections: 'Growing plants in the classroom', 'Greenhouse and school garden', 'Plant cultivation indoors', 'Plant propagation and notes on selected groups of plants'.

An evaluation of the Nuffield Junior Science Project was given by Ron Wastnedge* who was organizer of the project and is now an HMI. He was particularly enthusiastic about the interdisciplinary work which had resulted – the use of science as a reason for writing, and not only writing, but also painting, collage, sculpture or graphs. 'How else,' he asks, 'could a 10-year-old boy who

* In his article 'Whatever happened to Junior Science?' *Where* (July 1971).

100

has just walked to school through a grim north-eastern urban environment on a frosty morning be moved to write:

> This slightly frosted day
> Marks the solemn death of many plants
> A leafless nettle stands
> just as proud as ever
> without sting. And only a
> Dry leafless stem has it
> left to prove its existence
> The trodden grass leads to
> a patch of some more
> dried stalks – only plants.'

To somebody working within this philosophy, a prescribed course, work cards or kits would have been the very antithesis of what the children needed if they were to learn in the ways which they employ naturally and freely. This was why the two teachers' guides were written and why all attempts to induce the team to produce kits or sets of cards were resisted. Wastnedge felt that the work was supported by those who could accept an essentially Froebelian approach to learning: 'this meant the majority of teachers in infant schools, teachers in what are often called "forward looking" junior schools, as well as many college lecturers. To them it offered an extremely flexible approach to science, and it fitted easily into modern primary educational practice.' The project ended in 1966. It is worth pointing out that although a project's term has finished, its work carries on in its continuing influence. There is no doubt that Nuffield Junior Science has a good deal to offer the teacher of slow-learning children in secondary schools provided he or she is prepared to work through the teachers' guides and can accept the underlying philosophy. The proposal to integrate information derived from 'scientific' investigations with other subject areas, and to encourage the children to draw on all these sources when they are producing written or other creative work, has been explored by one of the present authors* with encouraging results.

Science 5–13

This project, directed by Len Ennever, and sponsored jointly by the Schools Council, the Nuffield Foundation and the Scottish Education Department, began work in 1967 and has produced books for teachers from 1970 onwards. These are published by Macdonald Educational. The project aimed to assist

* P. Widlake, 'Exploring the environment', *Educational Review*, Vol. 18, No. 1 (1965).

teachers to help children, through discovery methods, to gain experience and understanding of the environment and to develop their powers of thinking effectively about it.

Science 5–13 has *something* in common with Nuffield Junior Science and also with the two Nuffield secondary projects considered in this chapter, Nuffield Combined Science and Nuffield Secondary Science. This can be seen in the handbook, *With Objectives in Mind*, in which the authors set out their own educational convictions. In general, they felt children work best when trying to find answers to problems that they have themselves chosen to investigate. These problems are best drawn from their own environment and should be tackled largely by practical investigations, a view exactly in accord with Nuffield Junior Science. However, the style of presentation and the methods adopted by Science 5–13 in preparing the materials differed markedly from the other project.

In *With Objectives in Mind* the project has defined (with the help of teachers) 'Objectives for children learning science – guidelines to keep in mind', and these appear in each teachers' book. The general aim of developing an inquiring mind and a scientific approach to problems is broken down into eight general objectives: (1) developing interests, attitudes and aesthetic awareness; (2) observing, exploring and ordering observations; (3) developing basic concepts and logical thinking; (4) posing questions and devising experiments or investigations to answer them; (5) acquiring knowledge and learning skills; (6) communicating; (7) appreciating patterns and relationships; (8) interpreting findings critically. The project team has then taken the interesting step of specifying what developments in each of these aspects might be expected at three stages of mental development described in Piagetian terms: Stage 1 – intuitive; Stage 2 – concrete operational thinking; and Stage 3 – the transition to formal thought.

By making their objectives overt, the authors have invited discussion. Not everyone would be in agreement with all the items included in their analysis, and other scientists have, inevitably, criticized certain omissions, or doubted the validity of the whole enterprise. Len Ennever rather neatly anticipated these objections in the following quotations from the handbook: 'I've always thought that to define the aims of education in general terms is more or less meaningless; to do it more precisely is downright dangerous.' 'I am under no illusions about the difficulties of translating into action any high-sounding statements of aims and objectives. But these difficulties are minimal compared to the problems which the absence of such a guide creates.'

One obvious application of this analysis is as a source of reference for the teacher who wishes to increase his understanding of the thinking, concepts, skills, etc. which might be expected of older slow-learning children whose development is retarded in comparison with average pupils of their age. For example, by reading what is itemized for Stage 2 (the later stage of concrete operational thinking) one obtains an outline of what might be aimed for or expected under each of the broad aims. This would be a help in planning work for less successful pupils and would increase awareness of the difficulties of slower pupils.

The evaluation procedures produced a useful observation about slow learners – 'We found that in a class of mixed ability, there was a tendency for the work of the below-average groups to be strongly directed by the teacher, even if more able groups were allowed and encouraged to take responsibility for their own work and to work at their own pace. Now we find that if the whole class is below average, then they all have their work directed by the teacher. It must be very difficult for a teacher to avoid this, because slower children tend not to have ideas of their own about what they want to do. Nevertheless, directing their work is not the answer and teachers need a great deal of help to give them both understanding of and ideas of how to deal with this problem.'

Some examples of lessons from the units

Each unit consists of one or more books, and the material is related to different stages of educational development.

In *Coloured Things* the author reminds the teachers of the importance of thinking about objectives. For example, Stage 1 and Stage 2 objectives appropriate to this unit are quoted; two flow charts are given, one for 6- to 7-year-olds, the other for 8- to 9-year-olds. For the older group, the starting point was a discussion by the teacher of the colours the children used when painting. Arrows then indicate the manner in which topics grew from general discussion about colours into a consideration of coloured food and drink materials, coloured solutions, camouflage, investigating 'Action Man' in different combat suits, making models of aircraft camouflaged on runways, dinosaurs camouflaged in jungles, reading about other kinds of coloration.

The point is reiterated that children need wide general experience *whatever their age*. Some may linger long at this stage, others are soon ready to progress further. This obviously has application to older slow-learning children. A third flow chart then discusses work with 10- to 11-year-olds. This leads to work on road signs, car colours, stage lighting, tropical fish, precious stones, animal camouflage. It was felt that 'objectives could be used as a check that children are getting a balanced diet of experience.' For example, 'The fish group were working almost exclusively from books and so their work centred on objectives relating to acquiring knowledge and communicating. Perhaps they could be encouraged to branch out more . . . They might be guided into looking at live fish (can fish see colour?) or devise the experiment relating to the information they

103

have been recording. Or they might stay with their books, but their teacher, with a range of objectives in mind, could plan their future work along other lines.'

Chapter 2 ('Classroom colours') asks 'Why not start with the children themselves?', and begins by suggesting that the children look at themselves, look at their eyes and other children's eyes and hair. A West Indian girl noted, 'In my class there are white children, West Indians and Indians. I found that white children have these hair colours: blond, ginger, brown and black. West Indians have brown or black hair. Indians have black hair. White children have lots of different eyes. West Indians and Indians have brown eyes.' They were asked to look at skins, at hair (a diagram of a home-made microscope was included); they were asked to collect colours, plants and stones, glass and liquids, metals, papers and fabrics; to make colour lists, to set up a colour corner, to gather special collections, to classify colours. Changes in colour were studied through mixing paint, or examining transparent materials. Coloured solutions were then considered, moving on to coloured light, stage lighting, colour wheels.

In Chapter 3, 'Park and country colours' are discussed. In Chapter 4, 'Street colours' (looking at traffic and buildings) and in Chapter 5, 'Home colours' (looking at paints and papers, fabrics, food and drink and colour and heat).

Holes, Gaps and Cavities is another fascinating collection of ideas commencing with 'Looking for holes'. 'One of the best ways to start on holes is to collect some. It is not the number of holes collected that interests us here but rather that we will begin to look at holes more closely, questioning their function, and begin to gather starting points for further study.' The unit then goes on to discuss holes in the classroom, holes outdoors, making holes in paper, clay, knocking in nails, putting in screws, digging holes and drilling holes. The next section is entitled 'Holes and air'; then there is 'Flowing out of holes', 'Letting light through'; a topical heading 'Go and no go' (sieving); 'Holes in fabrics'; 'Holes in paper'; 'Filtering and straining'; 'Soils'. The final section is on 'Holes and natural objects' (holes in the head, holes in the skeleton, holes to live in, holes in plants).

Minibeasts deals with the creepy-crawlies of the invertebrate world and asks, 'Where can we find them, what are they, what do they do, can we keep them?'; there is an appendix on identification guidelines for teachers, a key to common pond animals and a second appendix on materials and equipment.

Structures and Forces has a separate unit for the cognitive Stages 1 and 2 and a separate unit for Stage 3. Stage 3, 'Forces moving things', is mostly about tensions. Part 2 has the following sub-headings: Tensions and compressions, Strength and shape, String experiments, Materials under tension, Surfaces of liquid, Capillarity, Structures and patterns.

104

For older children who are still at Stage 1 of educational development, adaptations of the unit *Early Experiences* could prove very useful. Every page has interesting things to do, illustrated with simple line-drawings and photographs to aid the non-technical.

Enough has been said, it is hoped, to support the feeling expressed by a number of teachers visited in their classrooms, that Science 5–13 can be the basis for much worth-while and enjoyable activity. There is no obligation to accept the authors' invitation to examine objectives, but the guidance is there for those teachers who wish to use it. In the meantime, those who require very practical suggestions for gainfully occupying even the slowest-learning child would do well to study the Science 5–13 materials with care. There are twenty-four titles in all.

Many LEAs have organized courses around the units and there is obviously a positive relationship between attendance at such a course and classroom achievement. Nothing is provided, however, except the units, so that the onus is on the teacher to acquire a range of materials likely to be used in the classroom situation. For the most part, these are homely objects like cotton-reels, bottles, milk-straws, bicycle pumps, paper cups, dress materials, but for more ambitious apparatus like a 'class wormery', a 'bird table' or an 'artificial cloud producer', access to a teachers' centre workshop might be desirable. This is *classroom science* and it is immensely encouraging to the non-specialist; there is nothing here dangerous or inhibiting. On the contrary, the likelihood of a simple model of a reciprocating engine (*Change*, Stages 1 and 2 and Background, page 38) being produced is considerably increased when one finds that nothing is required beyond cotton-reels, match-boxes and pins!

It is easy to exaggerate the level of sophistication achieved by some disadvantaged children. At one school, visited because of its involvement with the Humanities project, the art master rather shamefacedly pointed to a doll's house made from cardboard boxes. He said that fourth-year girls had spent weeks on it, coming back several evenings a week to work on it. It was very crude, really not much more than shoeboxes put together on a bungalow principle, but then it was decorated with wallpaper and fitted out with home-made furniture and generally cared for like a well-tended garden. It was genuine children's *work* and this degree of involvement is painfully rare among fifteen-year-old non-selective schoolgirls.

Many of the topics in the Science 5–13 materials offer similar possibilities to the teacher of disadvantaged children. This should not, of course, be construed as an argument against admitting these children to science laboratories or to science which has a secondary-school orientation. But it is well to bear in mind that the content and method of teaching cannot be decided merely by considering

105

what the teacher would like to achieve. It is also necessary to consider what pupils can best study in terms of the stage of development in their thinking.

S. Jackson* studied groups of children of both normal and sub-normal in-intelligence. His findings indicated that wide variations in levels of logical thinking may exist among children of similar ages and that the ability to think at a certain level in one situation does not necessarily imply an emergence of that level in other situations. Fifteen-year-old subjects of low intelligence achieved no higher levels of logical thinking than did 8-year-old pupils of average intelligence.

Many younger, and some older, secondary pupils will be unable to pose a hypothesis satisfactorily or to examine facts systematically, since their logical thinking will be tied to the concrete aspects of a given situation. The analysis of objectives in Science 5–13 should enable the alert teacher to identify activities suitable to the needs of such a child – even if he prefers to adapt more sophisticated materials for older pupils.

Nuffield Combined Science

The Nuffield O-level science courses were first planned in 1962. It was not found possible at that time to avoid the traditional divisions into physics, chemistry and biology but many teachers in schools felt the need for a combined science course. The Combined Science project (1965–69), directed by M. J. Elwell and based at the City of Birmingham College, was designed for children from 11 to 13 years of age across the whole ability range. The materials are published by Penguin Education and Longman.

Combined Science is a method of introducing children to natural phenomena and to ways in which the children themselves can interpret these phenomena. It is an attempt to recapture the unity of outlook and consistency of method which belong to the whole of science and which enable us to make reasoned statements about the world we live in.

The subject matter for Combined Science drew on the separate O-level science projects, but stands in its own right. It was a prime consideration that at some stage these individual sciences should be seen to constitute a unified whole, based on a common philosophy, with similar aims and methods. An introductory course affords a good opportunity for doing this when it is easier to draw on ideas and concepts from the various areas of science and bring them together in a meaningful way, free from artificial and contrived links. Following a careful analysis of the content, philosophy, and experimental approach of the O-level schemes, ten

* 'The growth of logical thinking in normal and sub-normal children', *British Journal of Educational Psychology*, Vol. 35 (1965), pp. 255–8.

topics were chosen to link together the material of the separate courses, and to unify as far as possible their different points of view and approaches. It was inevitable that in this process some of the sequences of work, as envisaged in the original schemes, would be modified to fit in with an overall view of science.

Combined Science is adaptable as an introduction to any subsequent work in science such as: separate Nuffield O-level courses, non-Nuffield O-level courses, Nuffield Secondary Science, work for the Certificate of Secondary Education, project work, or the Schools Council Integrated Science Project.

The authors emphasize that the general aim has been to produce a source of ideas, material and comment *to allow teachers to devise their own courses*. There is, deliberately, too much material so that the teacher must, of necessity, prepare a route diagram, based on a time allocation of five forty-minute periods a week. This should enable the pupils to develop concepts, to think and suggest things for themselves, to design experiments and activities to test their suggestions and allow them to learn from their mistakes, improving poor techniques by individual, specific comment there and then. Ready access to the apparatus is thus essential, but in the absence of a laboratory, an ordinary classroom can be converted at a reasonable cost. However, considerable attention has also been paid to extending children's work outside the laboratory, through suggestions for walks, visits and field-work.

It was felt that the best possible unification and reconciliation of the wide range of subject matter would be achieved by one teacher dealing with one class. To make this possible, a detailed teachers' guide in two parts has been prepared. There is a third part which contains a catalogue of teaching aids, apparatus details, apparatus construction sheets, hints, an appendix on mathematics teaching in relation to combined science, an apparatus index and a materials guide. To emphasize the teachers' active involvement, *Teachers' Guide I* and *Teachers' Guide II* have been produced in a form which allows for the inclusion of further notes, cuttings and so on, without breaking the back of the book. There are ten sections and for each there is a pupils' *Activities* booklet. Activities can be used to start children thinking about a new piece of work, to give them ideas of things to find out, to extend work done in the laboratory, to give some background to a piece of work, to take the place of class discussion, to give practical instructions both for home and laboratory-based experiments, and to give visual stimulation and reinforcement. There are also reference sheets which give children guidance on the use of items of apparatus such as burners, microscopes, and so on – these enable them to forge ahead without the delay of waiting for teacher's instructions. Background information will need to be supplemented by reference to books, such as those mentioned in the catalogue of teaching aids.

The ten sections are as follows:

A clearer picture may emerge if one section is given in detail.

d Trying to make crude naphthalene purer
e Is ink a single substance?
f Condensing the vapour from ink
g Demonstration distillation of ink
h Ink blots
i Investigating the green stuff in leaves

Sub-section 8   Using coloured substances from plants –
an introduction to acidity and alkalinity
a Making coloured extracts from plants
b Curing sourness
c Recognizing acid and alkaline substances
d Investigating the pH of water.

The arrangement of the teachers' guides and the statement of procedures and philosophy are clear and straightforward. The trials involved thirty-five schools, eighty teachers and 3000 children, and the materials reflect this thoroughness of approach. Indeed, it is all but impossible to fault the teachers' guides. They possess absolute clarity; the presentation of the numerous diagrams is elegant; they are successful in their use of coloured print to indicate different stages in the experiments and to present separately suggestions for possible extensions and modifications and quotations from teachers working with the trial materials. The guides seem expensive but they are a real credit to the publishers and a joy to use. There are also film loops (eighteen in colour and one black-and-white) with teaching notes.

Nuffield Secondary Science

Nuffield Secondary Science provides an integrated science course for all children of 13 to 16 who are unlikely to take O-level science. Work on the project started in 1965, the team at that time consisting of three full-time and two part-time members, and finished in 1970. The Director was Mrs Hilda Misselbrook and the project based at the Chelsea College of Science and Technology. The materials are published by Longman. This project stressed the importance of science teaching developing the quality of secondary- as opposed to primary-school work. The essence of Secondary Science, as of other school work with adolescents, is that it should be concerned with realistic matters of an adult stature. To quote the Newsom Report: 'To our boys and girls, realistic means belonging to the real world, that is the world of men and women, not schoolchildren.'*

* *Half our Future:* a report of the Central Advisory Council for Education (England) (HMSO, 1963), para. 321.

The Nuffield Secondary Science team stated in the foreword to the *Teacher's Guide* that they have never regarded their starting point as a limitation or as implying that the less able need a different kind of science. They have thought, rather, that the best way of bringing about improvement was by the development of a source of materials taken from all the sciences which the teacher can use with children of a wide range of ability.

Nuffield Secondary Science materials have been tested by over 10 000 boys and girls in England, Wales and Northern Ireland. They consist of a *Teacher's Guide*, an *Apparatus Guide* and eight theme texts. An additional volume on examining secondary science at CSE level is also available. Some thirty film loops, slides, half-tone illustrations and two background books have also been prepared as an integral part of the work. It is intended for approximately three-quarters of the pupils in secondary schools between 13 and 16. It offers teachers the chance to put into practice an approach to science teaching which the Newsom Report described as one of the major priorities for curriculum reform at this level. The themes are:

1. Interdependence of living things
2. Continuity of life
3. Biology of man
4. Harnessing energy
5. Extension of sense perception
6. Movement
7. Using materials
8. The earth and its place in the universe.

Each theme is broken down into what are called fields of study. It is possible to achieve differences in emphasis by selecting some fields of study for major treatment, some for minor treatment and by omitting others altogether. For example, under Theme 2, *Continuity of Life*, the fields of study are:

2.1 the manner of animal and plant reproduction and propagation;
2.2 inheritance;
2.3 process of evolution.

Under Theme 5, *Extension of Sense Perception*:

5.1 human limitations extending the range of sense perception;
5.2 hearing and the nature of sound;
5.3 seeing and the nature of light;
5.4 artificial aids to communication and recording.

The eight themes provide a 'quarry' from which teachers can build courses appropriate to their pupils' needs. Detailed suggestions to help teachers in the task of constructing appropriate courses or routes through the material, together with examples of possible routes, are given in Chapter 3 of the *Teachers' Guide*.

The bias throughout is extremely practical. We will take, as an example, the discussion on the use of worksheets. The *Teachers' Guide* defines these as a device by which the teacher helps a pupil to work as far as possible to his full capacity. It is not merely an instruction sheet with one or more precise instructions – it also asks questions which demand thought on many points. As far as possible, every worksheet should have one question to answer which makes the pupils think for themselves. Then there is a lengthy discussion of practical difficulties and suggestions for constructing worksheets. The problems considered include: ensuring that the worksheet is understood, ensuring that verbal communication takes place, encouraging literacy, planning worksheets, giving practice in visual communication.

Reactions of schools involved in Nuffield Combined Science and Secondary Science projects

1 *Extent of use with disadvantaged children*

Some of the schools which replied to our questionnaire were using the materials only 'down to' groups who could cope with a CSE Mode III course (say the top eight of twelve forms).

Midlands 11 to 18 comprehensive school
The school was invited to take part as a trial school in the O-level projects in physics, chemistry and biology in 1964. In physics and chemistry we have expanded the project to cover all pupils taking O level in these subjects and these pupils sit Nuffield G CE examinations. We have also developed our own CSE Mode III courses in these two subjects on Nuffield lines. The school also took part in the original trials for the Combined Science project in 1966. This applied to the top eight forms (out of twelve) in Lower School (11 to 13 years). We continue with this project as it serves as the basis for the introduction of the Nuffield work in the separate sciences in the third year.

North-eastern 11 to 18 comprehensive school
Nuffield Combined Science Project is being used throughout the streamed classes of the first and second years including disadvantaged children. The Nuffield Secondary Science Project is being used in all streamed classes in the third and fourth year, including disadvantaged pupils.

111

Shropshire 11 to 16 secondary boys' school
The Nuffield Secondary Science Project is used in all the streamed classes in third and fourth year, including the disadvantaged pupils.

This still left a substantial number of schools which had received the materials with enthusiasm and attempted to use them with the bottom 20 per cent of the ability range.

Lincolnshire 11 to 18 comprehensive school
There is a wealth of material which is suitable as it stands but modification of worksheet suggestions is essential with the less able children. Some of the more sophisticated investigations need careful teaching but our lower-ability children have found much of interest and have been taken through some material which we would not have thought of teaching before the advent of Nuffield Secondary Science.

One science adviser considered that Nuffield Science had transformed the teaching of his subject so far as the least able were concerned:

I have to hand the comments of four teachers, two of whom are dealing with the Secondary Science Project (13 to 16 age group) and two with the Combined Science Project (11 to 13 age group). Individual opinions will, of course, be coloured by personal teaching attitudes and ability. It must also be stressed that my sample has had to be very limited since few of the schools involved in Nuffield work have distinct ability streams. The replies are from teachers who take sets of backward children.
In general it would appear that both projects are successful with the bottom 20 per cent. Reasons given are their relevance to life, and that they are pupil-based in outlook, and sufficient apparatus has been made available to make investigations interesting.
In all cases much adaptation of the materials has been necessary involving leaving out difficult concepts, avoiding mathematics where possible, producing *simple* worksheets and using direct teaching if it has been found that 'circus' arrangements are too confusing.
Also what comes out is that the teachers have been surprised by the degree of interest in topics which previously they might have thought too difficult. The students have risen to the occasion to the best of their ability. Undoubtedly, some of the Nuffield Secondary Science materials will be significant for the least able pupils when the school leaving age is raised, but there is plenty of evidence that both projects will prove progressively helpful across the whole 11 to 16 age and ability bands.

112

The style of organization adopted by schools in order to accommodate the bottom 20 per cent differed considerably. Most favoured homogeneous ability groups:

Midlands 11 to 18 comprehensive school
A diluted form of the Combined Science course is taken by the lower-ability groups in Lower School. For these groups, of homogeneous ability, worksheets are prepared carefully and are used for guidance in practical work and for simple follow-up work. For third-year pupils, no specific Nuffield course operates for the lower-ability range (bottom 20 per cent) but those who continue for a full fourth year often find themselves in a group leading to CSE Mode III in physics and/or chemistry, in which case the group will be of mixed ability. With the raising of the school leaving age, we are already taking steps to use material from the Nuffield Secondary Science courses for those pupils of lower attainment and to develop a course from the third year onwards. Again we are hoping to use worksheets.

Lincolnshire 11 to 18 comprehensive school
We teach streamed groups with a 'special group' of remedial children removed. The streams are established on ability in science in the first three years in the school but in the fourth and fifth years the groups became mixed ability by virtue of options chosen by the pupils quite freely. It has been true in the past that these groups have tended towards the higher abilities but we have had children from all ability ranges taking CSE Mode III. After RoSLA these groups will tend towards a fuller cross-section of ability.

Cardiff 11 to 16 high school (mixed)
Yes, this material has been used extensively with the bottom 20 per cent. Pupils have, in fact, worked with others of similar ability levels but are frequently observed helping less able classmates. They have handled very expensive equipment with great care.

Yorkshire 11 to 18 comprehensive school
The remedial class is taught as one group for science. They work in pairs of their own choosing and are allowed to change partners if they so wish.

A few schools were making arrangements for what they called 'mixed-ability groups'. In one, the first year were organized into mixed-ability groups, the second year into three broad bands covering the whole range. In another, the more able helped the less able – but the teacher thought there was a risk that the former did all the work.

2 Work in the laboratory

For those who have not previously observed work in which the pupils are involved in their own investigations, a visit to a laboratory where the teachers are enthusiasts about this approach is an exhilarating experience. In both Nuffield Combined Science and Nuffield Secondary Science, the experimental work is often designed as a 'circus' in which the pupils, usually working in pairs, move freely from one experimental situation to another. Complex and expensive apparatus is freely handled by all ability groups, and the amount of damage done is not excessive. Every pupil has the chance to become actively involved in science, actually to handle apparatus such as a circuit-board and to explore it for himself, in his own way and at his own conceptual level.

Midlands 11 to 18 comprehensive school (first-year group). Circuit-boards involve the use of a large number of easily losable bits and pieces but we saw children working readily in pairs, spread out to all corners of a spacious laboratory. Although this arrangement afforded ample opportunities for time-wasting or damage, this did not happen. It was, in fact, a most impressive class. The girls seemed to be enjoying it as much as the boys. The lesson was in two parts. In the first, the children were allowed to experiment with the boards, to set up and break the circuits as they chose. When this period seemed to be drawing to an end of its own accord, the remedial teacher issued worksheets with diagrams which had to be copied and a hypothesis to be tested, namely: will the bulb light when this wiring arrangement is adopted? The recording was done simply through a yes/no worksheet. Most pupils had no difficulty understanding what was required in so far as the recording was concerned but when, on several occasions, they were not able to match the diagram from the visual symbols, the teacher taught them by orientating the circuit-boards – marking in the wires on the diagram in the same colour as the leads on the circuit-board, and verbalizing. In this way, all the children with difficulties resolved them and most of them completed the assignments. Most impressive was the hum of activity, the degree of involvement, the way in which children kept coming to the teacher and saying, 'Look, it works; it lights', and the general feeling that they were happily and actively engaged in cognitive tasks which were a little bit ahead of their previous attainment.

Midlands middle school, 9 to 13. At a middle school, we observed a class which was investigating the filtration of naphthalene. The children had been working on solutions and for homework had described their previous work with salt. They were now given a brief introduction to naphthalene and invited to attempt

114

to discover how to purify it. They were in possession of the method as they had carried out the same operation with common salt. Trays of apparatus were issued, one to each of six groups. There was no fuss and bother, one member of each group collected the tray, and they worked in groups of four. They spent the best part of a period attempting to dissolve naphthalene first in cold water and then in hot water. Hot water was boiled in a kettle and carried from the front to the groups without any mishap. They began to observe that the chemical would not dissolve, though this took a considerable time. One group having tried to pass the liquid through a filter paper concluded that the filter paper had a hole in it and did it again. Eventually, the teacher began to drop hints that naphthalene was tar and how did you get tar off your clothes if you had put some there? Methylated spirit was mentioned and this was available. At last, somebody said outright that naphthalene would not dissolve in water and with a little guidance from the teacher made the suggestion that they try methylated spirit. Once one group had got this far, the others began to note and follow. Soon, one or two groups had completed the experiment and produced a purified form of naphthalene – white flakes compared with the yellowish-brown of its polluted state.

Another lesson was concerned with heating things. Each group had a Bunsen burner and recorded what happened when various substances were heated. There was a sub-group in this lesson, consisting of slower children who had been sent in for experience, and these were examining insects under the microscope and enjoying themselves very considerably. Having examined the insect, they then attempted to draw it.

An inner-city 11 to 18 comprehensive school, Lancashire. A comprehensive school abutting a depressed, inner-city neighbourhood, had built its science round the Nuffield teachers' guides. The head of department had been involved from the early stages and had attended in-service training in the city. He was an exceptionally able teacher who devoted himself wholeheartedly to the job. He conceived the role of head of department as a very active one. His system for helping probationary teachers was to split the class into two parts and to take one half in what amounted to a demonstration lesson, while the less experienced teacher imitated him with the other half of the class.

Very detailed syllabuses had been prepared and the department as a whole was closely controlled by its head. He considered that this kind of structured approach was the best for teachers at the beginning of their career. They were given firm indications of what to do and how to do it, and could discard this or attempt work of their own at a later stage. The two young teachers with whom we lunched expressed much appreciation for this kind of guidance.

The department was making a genuine effort to teach science to all ability groups. The recording was done on pre-prepared worksheets which reduced the amount of writing required to a minimum. Inspection of these indicated that some pupils with very considerable writing disabilities were able to attempt the work and to answer questions even though the vocabulary load would seem to be excessive. This was achieved by much oral preparation and by organizing the pupils into circuses so that the less able pupil could consult with the more able. In this way, the reading difficulty seemed largely to have been overcome. The worksheets were liberally illustrated so that the amount of recording to be done had been kept to a minimum.

Some examples of errors indicating learning disabilities were: 'because you get week when you do it for 100 secsonds you og slower', 'oxeger' for 'oxygen', 'samll muscles'.

This teacher told us how well some of these pupils were doing in their science work and that he had been surprised when he saw the IQ scores at a later date: he found they were very low and would not have expected work of this quality from pupils who scored in that IQ range.

Modifications of the materials in Nuffield Combined Science and Secondary Science

1 *Need for modification*

The schools generally considered most of the material to be suitable in its existing form. A Cardiff school had found that the main problem had been to produce suitable workcards and worksheets for the less able children. A Shropshire comprehensive school concurred:

> Work has to be presented visually and orally. Written instructions are brief. Worksheets are used very little as they can cause frustration. Long-term objectives mean little to these pupils – so short-term objectives are posed so that success is reinforced. Actual Nuffield Secondary Science material has not been altered very much.

A Birmingham comprehensive school had also made modifications, mainly by selection (as indeed, the teachers' guides urge them to do):

> Combined Science has been used as a source rather than a course. We would not be able to cover all of Combined Science in two years because of the lower level of ability of our pupils and because of the time allocation of two 70-minute periods per week. We teach about two-thirds of the material. The approach is as recommended in the texts. Much modification is needed for the bottom stream. The bottom stream are able to cope adequately with most of the practical work, but careful selection is needed to ensure that the

116

concepts developed are possible for them. All of their course is derived from the Combined Science course but written work is kept to a minimum with much help being given with recording. The emphasis is placed on individual and class discussion.

2 *Worksheets*

There was a considerable difference of opinion about the importance of worksheets. A Staffordshire school thought that worksheets of any kind were contrary to the Nuffield spirit. A Worcestershire school, on the other hand, thought the whole success of the approach depended upon the provision of duplicated material and wanted extra clerical help for this purpose. On the whole, those teachers who had studied the performance of their disadvantaged pupils, and tried to produce worksheets which relied as much as possible on non-verbal cueing and open-ended questions, seemed most successful.

As the worksheet examples on pp. 118 and 119 show, even in simplified sheets it is difficult to avoid words which present difficulty to poor readers. Thus, in examples 1 and 2 we have 'crystals', 'vapour', 'condensed', 'liquid', 'parallel', 'circuit', 'series' – words which are unlikely to have been met in remedial reading books. Some of these words would not yield easily to attempts to 'sound' them out, even if the pupil had acquired some phonic skills. Drawing attention to these words, getting the pupils to list them and to learn them in remedial reading sessions would help. Some 'technical' words would be suitable for learning through the making of a science picture-dictionary. There are other words ('removed', 'separately', 'compared', 'experiment', 'insert', 'filtered', 'heated') which illustrate the need to continue word study identifying common spelling patterns, beginnings and endings (-er, re-, ex-, in-, -ed, -ing).

3 *Audio-visual aids*

We observed many lessons where backward boys and girls were admitted to all the resources of the laboratory, but there were few instances of systematic preparation for science lessons – yet this is obviously an 'intervention procedure' within the normal scope of any English or remedial department. One would expect science teachers to be enthusiastic about the use of audio-visual devices but few schools appeared to use tape-recorders and head-sets to overcome the reading problem. Ian Townsend* has argued powerfully in favour of educational

* 'Science for the special child: Part I, Introduction and definition' and 'Part II, Development of some appropriate techniques', *School Science Review*, Vol. 52, No. 181 (June 1971) and Vol. 53, No. 184 (March 1972).

Example 1

PROCEDURE

We heated some blue copper sulphate crystals in a test-tube as shown in the diagram below. White powder was left. The vapour given off condensed (changed to liquid) as it cooled in passing down the condensing tube. Clear liquid was collected in the test-tube.

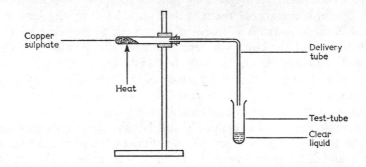

RESULTS

Before we could say the clear liquid was water we had to decide on some tests. Say what these were and what results we got.

_____

_____

_____

_____

CONCLUSIONS

From the results of our tests we can say that the clear liquid is _____

Note:

1. When you added a little water to the white copper sulphate did you expect it to get hotter or colder? _____

2. Did it get hotter or colder? _____

3. Explain why. _____

_____

118

Example 2

Check that all your links are tight before each experiment and remember to take out a link before you insert a meter.

5. Current going into bulb B.
   (Note: you need to move bulb B.)

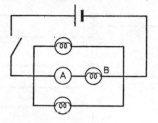

6. Current coming out of bulb B.
   (Note: you move bulb B back.)

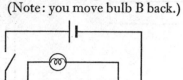
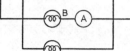
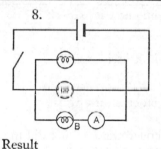

Result _____

Result _____

7.

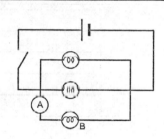

8.

Result _____

Result _____

CONCLUSIONS

(i) What have you learnt about what happens when one bulb is removed from a parallel circuit?

_____

(ii) How is this different from removing one bulb from a series circuit?

_____

(iii) What can you say about the current going into and coming out of any one bulb?

_____

(iv) What can you say about the current going into each bulb separately?

_____

(v) What can you say about the total current going into all three bulbs compared to the current going into each separately?

_____

119

Example 3

SALT FROM ROCK SALT

What colour was the rock?

How did you know it had salt in?

What was in it besides salt?

Why did you crush it up?

Next you added water. What did the salt do?

Then you filtered it – what was left in the filter paper?

The clear water which came through the filter paper had the

_____ in it.

You heated the salty water and the water _____ into the air.

Pure salt was left in the dish.

120

technology for the 'special' child. He gave a host of practical examples, based on his classroom experience and reported: 'I am continually getting requests from the children to have "more of those tape things".' He used both audio and visual materials, separately and in combination, and his splendid articles give full details of what was done and how to do it. But, as he cogently concludes:

> The important thing is not that new approaches to learning are being developed. The important thing is that children enjoy their science, so that it makes some contribution – no matter how small – to their development as mature adults. In face of this, everything else is irrelevant.

4 *Testing techniques for disadvantaged pupils*

Though backward pupils may have enjoyed and learnt from their science lessons, they may be defeated by traditional examinations. They cannot cope with the handwriting required; they cannot organize their knowledge quickly and coherently enough, and often they cannot read the questions or grasp their significance. One school had attempted to overcome the examination problem in an interesting way. The same paper was set for the whole year group and they were graded right across the year, but the remedial class answered their paper *orally*. The science teacher took them into the language laboratory and explained in detail what was required; then each question was put to the pupils orally and they taped their answers. To obtain the full flavour of their replies, it is, of course, necessary to hear their voices, with their delicious variety of intonation. But some idea of the original can be obtained from a transcript.

Question 1. From *each* of the following four lists choose the ONE item which you consider to be the 'odd man out'. Write down its name and give your reason for your choice:

(a) brass, glass, grass;
(b) daisy, rose, twig, stone, mushroom, wheat, seaweed;
(c) daisy, spider, daffodil, snake, salt, mouse, fern, crab, whale;
(d) chalk, water, air, aluminium, iron, oil, lead, mercury, asbestos, tadpole, rubber, brick.

Question 2. From *each* of the following lists choose the TWO things which have most in common. Write them down and give the reasons for your answer.

(a) dog, earthworm, horse;
(b) tiger, earwig, lobster;
(c) elephant, spider, mushroom;
(d) cat, dog, goldfish;

(e) crocodile, lion, tortoise;
(f) bear, oyster, snail;
(g) bear, oyster, whale;
(h) iron, copper, chalk, rubber;
(i) tadpole, frog, goldfish;
(j) crab, goldfish, spider;
(k) aluminium, copper, brass.

Answers

I think that I've picked grass because it's softer than all the rest and the others aren't soft.

I think that I've picked stone because all the others grow like themselves and stone is formed on its own with the rock.

I think salt because all the others are either an animal or a flower.

I've picked water because water is the only one that you can drink, and none of the others you can't drink.

I've picked dog and horse because you can have a dog and a horse more of a pet than an earthworm.

I've picked earwig and lobster because they're both quite small animals and they're much smaller than a tiger . . . and you see a tiger in the zoo and you don't see a lobster and an earwig.

Elephants and spider are a sort of an animal but a mushroom, it just grows in the garden and in wild places.

I've picked a cat and a dog because if you have a cat and a dog it doesn't have to live in water, but if you had a goldfish it has to live in water or else it will die.

Certainly, the tapes scotched any suggestion that these were non-verbal children. Many of their answers were thoroughly adequate and yet, if they had been required to write them, they would all have received an E grade. Naturally, few reached the top 25 percentile but the teacher pointed out that many of them had scored C, a grade which would have been completely beyond their capabilities had it been a written examination. Thus they were able to compare grades with the top streams and some of them were obtaining marks equivalent to those of the more able, which was obviously very good for their morale. The teacher was not of the opinion that the A stream would have raised their grades pro-

portionately had *they* been allowed to record, because the difference between written attainment and verbal in their case was less dramatic.

Ian Townsend, in the articles quoted above, gave examples of multiple-choice questions administered by tape: 'lots of simple questions to give the child a better chance and higher score.'

The most sophisticated account of oral testing in science is contained in Schools Council Examinations Bulletin 21 – *CSE: an Experiment in the Oral Examining of Chemistry* (Evans/Methuen Educational, 1971). This investigation found that the oral examination had 'a reasonably high reliability and a reasonably high validity' and was interesting and potentially valuable. It was felt that an oral examination could serve as an instrument of external moderation and as a satisfactory method of assessment for those schools choosing the Mode II or Mode III forms of examination. The amount of equipment needed and the time and organization required are drawbacks within the school situation.

Conclusions

1. The various science projects reviewed in this chapter have immediate relevance to teachers of disadvantaged children.

2. The teachers' guides produced by the Nuffield Combined Science and Nuffield Secondary Science projects provide excellent models for projects in other subjects, especially those concerned with disadvantaged pupils for whom this 'guided discovery' approach is highly relevant.

3. The list of objectives given in Science 5–13 provides a useful check-list for teachers wishing to analyse their classroom practice. This project goes further, however, by suggesting activities appropriate to different levels of mental functioning, and the various guides would be useful for teachers of slow learners in secondary schools. Teachers in special schools would find the guides of particular value in developing science activities with the most backward pupils.

4. Some of the most ambitious and successful teaching of disadvantaged children which we have observed was undertaken by science teachers. This should not be allowed to mask the widespread neglect of the subject with these pupils.

5. Audio-visual techniques widely used in remedial and special education, if applied to science, would considerably enlarge the number of pupils who could participate.

123

VIII. Mathematics

It is not so long ago that secondary mathematics for slow learners was a dull continuation of practice of arithmetical facts and processes which they had not mastered at the primary stage, enlivened with some 'practical' arithmetic, and in the older age groups with work on social arithmetic – hire-purchase, budgeting, etc. No doubt this approach still lingers on in spite of the great changes in mathematics teaching. Some of the projects and materials referred to in this chapter offer ways of making mathematical experiences more interesting and profitable for slow-learning and disadvantaged children. We have attempted to assess how far these approaches are being used with slow learners and how appropriate they are.

The very first Schools Council Curriculum Bulletin *Mathematics in Primary Schools** reflected changes in the aims and methods of mathematics which had been developing for some time, stimulated by the studies of Piaget and by other developments such as those associated with Stern and Dienes. While discovery methods were advocated in *Mathematics in Primary Schools*, there was full awareness of the importance of sequence and continuity: 'such mathematical opportunities as arise naturally in the classroom, though excellent in themselves as a continuation or extension of earlier experience, are rarely sufficient and broad enough even at this stage. We, as teachers, shall need to provide the right kind of experience to serve as a basis for more systematic learning.'

Excellent advice on classroom procedures is given in Chapters 7 and 9 ('Classroom problems' and 'Straight from the classroom'); and the mathematical procedures summarized in Chapter 5 ('Children, shapes and space') and Chapter 6 ('The place of graphical representation in the learning of mathematics') can readily be adapted to the needs of disadvantaged pupils. Children of very varied abilities can represent graphically the results of their own investigations and experiments. By this means, they can see relationships between the variables concerned which they would not otherwise be able to appreciate. Most teachers will have experimented with curve-stitching, one of several techniques which allow the concrete representation of relationship graphs; they will know that these activities appeal to pupils of all abilities.

This Curriculum Bulletin can be recommended as an introduction to the

* HMSO, 1965; 4th edn 1972.

methods of teaching primary mathematics which are relevant to many older backward pupils. Some of the projects referred to later suggest topics and methods suited to older pupils' interests and age.

Nuffield Primary Mathematics

The Nuffield Primary Mathematics Project (1964–71), under the direction of Professor G. Matthews, took up the work of preparing teachers' guides and has produced a very practical series (published by W. & R. Chambers and John Murray) covering three main topics:

> Computation and structure
> Shape and size
> Pictorial representation and graphs leading to algebra.

The aim of the project was to devise a contemporary approach to mathematics for children from 5 to 13. The teachers' guides (no pupils' materials have been produced at primary level)* do not comprise an entirely new syllabus. The stress is on how to learn not on what to teach. Running through all the work is the central notion that the children must be free to make their own discoveries and think for themselves. To achieve understanding young children cannot go straight to abstractions — they need to handle things ('apparatus' is too grand a word for at least some of the equipment concerned — conkers, beads, scales, globes, and so on).

From the beginning the project eschewed novelty for its own sake. Any topical aspect of the subject introduced had to be more intelligible and purposeful (and so easier to teach) than that which it replaced. Perhaps the most important message of 'modern' mathematics, it was suggested in Curriculum Bulletin 1, is its ubiquity, the fact that doing sums is only a fraction of the programme envisaged.

The full list of teachers' guides is almost a mathematics syllabus in itself; this project has also produced *Into Secondary School*, reminding teachers that much of its work is appropriate to middle- and secondary-school pupils.

The teachers' guides were conceived on the assumption that they would become 'set books' for in-service training courses at teachers' centres, where facilities would also exist for making apparatus and for the teachers themselves to learn through discovery methods. The guides are certainly well adapted to these purposes; *Shape and Size* provides typical examples of the presentation of materials.

* Pupil materials for use in middle schools or the first two years of secondary school are now being published. Details are given in Appendix B.

125

A group of children will have, say, twenty-four of each shape of brick or block of a given size (cube, cuboid, prism, cylinder, etc.).

> Use all the blocks of one kind.
> Try to build a wall which has at least two thicknesses of brick.
> Do this with all the shapes. You may put the bricks in any pattern you wish.
> Which shapes did you find were the easiest for building walls?
> Why do you think this is?

The children should have found that the cube- and rectangular-shaped bricks were the best. This is because these bricks can occupy the same place in several ways. They have 'square corners' and parallel faces which fit together, and opposite faces of the same shape and size. House bricks, toy building bricks, constructional games use these shapes for this reason. Children will come across many examples, particularly in their toys and games, and so these 'regular' shapes are considered before irregular shapes.

Professor Matthews has defined mathematics as 'the capacity to transfer from one situation to another'.* Whitehead is quoted with approval: 'the whole of mathematics consists in the organization of a series of aids to the imagination in the process of reasoning.' This large view of mathematics permeates the teachers' guides. The mathematical imagination cannot be stimulated within a straitjacket provided by an approved syllabus: 'the only serious message I have is "end exams".' Professor Matthews warned against the 'package deal': 'the most idiotic card I have seen is one which says "take two lots of weights and prove that 2 lb equals 32 oz" . . . I should beware of all hardware. Let us by all means use television and so on but do let us remember that maths has to do with people.'

We have received little evidence that Nuffield Primary Mathematics has been used with backward secondary children though the approach would seem very appropriate for pupils in first- and second-year remedial streams who will certainly not all have progressed through the work normally achieved by average juniors.

* Schools Council Working Paper No. 22, *The Middle Years of Schooling from 8 to 13* (HMSO, 1969).

Midland Mathematics Experiment

Although the mathematics approaches discussed so far have obvious application to older disadvantaged pupils, the earliest project concerned specifically with this population was the Midland Mathematics Experiment. The experiment was initiated in 1961; it was directed by C. Hope at Worcester College of Education until 1972, and since then by R. M. Stokes at Coventry College of Education. The project received a Schools Council grant for part of its work, for the three years 1968–71. The materials are published by Harrap. From the beginning the project involved practising teachers. Although its brief has included GCE A level (and topic booklets for A-level work have been produced by the project), complete GCE O-level and CSE courses have been published, and there is an anthology in two volumes of non-examination mathematics under the title *Excursions from Mathematics*. This book grew out of a deep concern for children who are now classified as Newsom, i.e. those children who do not normally take external examinations.

The teachers who wrote this book claimed that the entire contents arose out of classroom experience with children of less than average ability and that in all cases the work had been done with children; 'the pupils have been the centre of the development and the scheme of work has grown out of the success and interest of the children concerned.' They felt that 'it is important that all pupils and especially the less able ones may grow to understand the ways in which mathematical reasoning underlies the organization and administration governing the lives of people who work.'

The non-examination course was in six parts: 1. Number; 2. Area; 3. Transformations; 4. Statistics; 5. Topics; 6. Mathematical methods. Many of the suggestions would be recognized by a teacher familiar with Nuffield mathematics. This particularly applies to the section on Number which includes such items as magic number cards, number patterns, relations, and a section on suggestions for further uses of Cuisenaire rods. Section 6 includes: job analysis, magic squares and linear programming, critical path analysis, flow diagrams, market survey and consumer research.

Even though the material was prepared on the basis of classroom experience, the amount of reading matter and the style of presentation would be difficult for many disadvantaged pupils. However, like so much of the work observed in the classroom, it soon became apparent that a good teacher could use this as source material, which he or she would adapt to particular requirements. It was also a source of some surprise to find that within the groups observed many children were capable of following a quite complex text provided that they were

127

given careful guidance and encouraged to use a dictionary, and were given adequate preparation and perhaps a vocabulary list.

In the one class, children were working from the O-level text and were successfully completing the section on navigation. The teacher encouraged the more able to help the least able; and, of course, it was apparent here, as elsewhere, that the remedial stream contained a very wide range of ability and attainment. For some of them orientation problems were difficult. For example, 'If you are facing east and you turn a quarter-turn to your left, what direction are you now facing?' or 'If you are facing north and you turn through half a complete turn to your right, what direction do you now face?' The teacher, however, began by requiring the children to stand holding a ruler with which they pointed north; they carried out the turns physically, and with this preparation most of the children proved able to work through a quite complex series of exercises. It was most impressive that the children worked quietly while the teacher talked to the visitor and when the bell went for the end of the first lesson there was a quite spontaneous groan.

One child observed had marked difficulty with written work. In exercises concerned with sets she had collected pictures of various articles and under one group she wrote, 'Two parr of tousers to wiar'. Underneath a collection of shapes she wrote, 'And there shapes aleve got sate londs and I have over doud these shapes we a pencil.' Perusal of her work showed that, though her ability in written work was a great handicap, she had nevertheless covered a wide range of topics with a reasonable degree of understanding. In some tasks such as symmetry pattern-making and graphs, her work was neat and of a good standard. She coped well with exercises concerning 'turns' and was able to plot a route on a given grid even though this involved numerous changes of direction. She participated with enjoyment in work on the binary scale, and simple work involving activities around such topics as navigation and computers. What could easily have been a 'failure' subject for her was in fact one she enjoyed and she was able to participate in activities derived from quite difficult mathematical concepts.

Few teachers of disadvantaged pupils consider it desirable to work rigidly to a prescribed syllabus. They base their work upon a scheme such as the Midland Mathematics Experiment materials provide, but seize every opportunity to pursue interest as it is manifested, and follow television programmes or other possible sources of interest. In the view of one teacher there were a number of ways in which this approach helped. It enabled her to establish new relationships with her girls and sometimes with parents; it helped to build up confidence because it led to discussion with others and to a class organization based around groups. 'Consequently, the girls are learning to assess, plan and think ahead, looking for pitfalls and snags – this carries through to other work.' The project represented a new approach: it presented problems and ideas that do not work out – 'I was taught that in maths you were right or wrong, and that problems *had* to work out, sometimes with a remainder! Now the girls find that the problems don't always work out – they can go so far and no further – just as in real life.' This notion of approximation was completely new to most of the girls. Rote learning of tables was not emphasized. In the teacher's view, if they had not learned their tables by secondary age, there was little point in wasting time by prolonging the agony. Tables were therefore pasted into the backs of books on the grounds that they would be using ready-reckoners, adding machines and the like when they left school. Even so, it was surprising how many girls knew their tables after working through the section on 'Number'.

Part of the success of this work was due to the teacher's insistence on activity. Opportunities were taken to do art-work – illustrating topics with picture-making, making mobiles, cutting out illustrations from colour magazines and displaying work in interesting ways.

The binary scale gave the chance to punch holes as in proper tapes and the class was able to 'play' with a computer that someone's husband kindly made for them – a crude but effective piece of apparatus. This was followed by finger-counting and by the time this topic had been exhausted, the second section had kept them occupied for nearly two terms. The class had looked at the history of counting and this had led on to a project with ideas coming from the television programme 'Blue Peter' for making the beads on the Japanese soroban. This soroban led to one of the girls constructing her own binary computer.

Enough has been written, it is hoped, to support the view that the Midland Mathematics Experiment is an excellent source of stimulating mathematical ideas. A teacher who is willing to learn alongside the pupils will find that there is much here to inspire and delight them both.

Mathematics for the Majority

This five-year project, under the direction of Philip Floyd and based at the University of Exeter, ended in April 1972. The materials are published by Chatto & Windus Educational. The main aim was to produce a series of teachers' guides which would lead teachers to reassess their work in mathematics with pupils between 13 and 16 years of age and of average and below average ability, and provide source materials and ideas from which these teachers could make up their own courses.

In Schools Council Working Paper No. 14, *Mathematics for the Majority: a Programme in Mathematics for the Young School Leaver,*[*] Philip Floyd defined

* HMSO, 1967.

the ability range to be considered as that of pupils of average and below average ability in mathematics. Grade 4 CSE pass was taken as an upper limit and the lower limit was rather indeterminate, stopping short of children receiving specialized remedial treatment in special schools or classes. 'We are to consider then something in the order of one half of the pupils in secondary modern schools and the equivalent ability range in comprehensive schools, from the age of 13 onwards up to 16.'

Reviewing the projects then current in Britain, Floyd concluded that none of them was answering the needs of the less able pupils. It was suggested by some that rewritten editions of some teaching materials with much the same content, but presented somewhat differently, might make them acceptable in some quarters for pupils with a slower rate of progress. The problem here was the amount of work required of the teacher if the suggestions were to be carried out and the timing suggested by the text extended, e.g. one book of the text would be carried over two years instead of one: 'the onus is then on the class teacher to provide suitable and adequate material which is purposeful, interesting and relevant.'

> Whilst the manifest difficulties of the present situation – shortage of mathematically qualified staff, indifferent or even poor teaching facilities, inadequate or inappropriate equipment – apply in some measure to all pupils in the secondary modern schools, they bear particularly heavily on the children in the lower ability ranges. Some teachers of the slower learners, even though self-confessed non-mathematicians, have primary school training and experience which is often to their advantage when teaching such children. In matters of approach and method there is much to be learned by the secondary teacher from modern advances in primary school mathematics teaching. A mere copying of them might well prove inadequate for the older pupil, but modifications and adaptations might quite well allow the slower learning child to travel along a truly mathematical road as far as his ability permits and at his individual rate of progress . . .

Floyd then delivered a caveat with which the present survey would like to be associated:

> The amount of space devoted to some enterprising highlights, by no means unique but not as common as they might be, must not be allowed to mask the dreary dullness of what is nearer the norm in the matter. All too often the mathematics met at the level of this study is a mysterious, solemn ritual at best, and at worst it is a dose of rather nasty medicine to be taken at regular intervals, allegedly for the good of the pupil.

130

The mathematical priorities which were delineated as a result of this analysis were as follows:

(a) *Experiences of mathematical situations* which will encourage powers of judgement and the exercise of imagination, and which will enable the pupil to apply his limited techniques to real situations . . .

(b) *Some understanding of a number of mathematical concepts* and some effectiveness in using some techniques in areas of knowledge which appear basic if the pupil is to take a responsible and intelligent part as a member of society . . .

(c) *Experiences of mathematics combined with other aspects of the curriculum* in a variety of situations relevant to the interests of the pupils and the world in which they live . . .

(d) . . . to give the pupil at an appropriate intellectual level some *appreciation of order and pattern* in the man-made world.

This was one of four projects which attempted to define its 'target population'. In an article in the *Times Educational Supplement*, Philip Floyd described a sample of 602 fourth-year pupils in fifteen secondary schools. They were drawn from the lowest streams yet they obtained a mean non-verbal intelligence test quotient of 89·3. The mean reading age was 10·6 and the mean mathematical age 9·9. While these scores indicate a considerable retardation in attainment, it was also found that the spread of scores was wide, some pupils in those low streams achieving quite a high level. While the scores clearly show the academic weakness of these pupils, the relatively high non-verbal score and the wide spread of attainment scores suggest that expectations for achievement and the kind of work to which pupils might be capable of responding should not be narrow and limited. An 'attitude-to-mathematics' test was given and showed a significant deterioration in attitudes from the third to the fourth year.

Fifty-five per cent of teachers teaching mathematics to fourth-year pupils were non-specialists. The Mathematics for the Majority Project was intended to be a means of helping such teachers. As the introduction to one of the teachers' guides said: 'the project was set up to help teachers construct courses for pupils of average and below average ability that relate mathematics to their experience and provide them with some insight into the processes that lie behind the use of mathematics as the language of science and as a source of interest in everyday things.' The following list of titles of guides gives some indication of the topics covered: *Mathematical Experience; Machines, Mechanisms and Mathematics; Assignment Systems; Number Appreciation; Mathematical Pattern; Mathematics from Outdoors; Luck and Judgement; From Counting to Calculating.* (Other guides published since the end of the survey are: *Some Simple Functions;*

131

Algebra of a Sort; Geometry for Enjoyment; Space Travel and Mathematics, Vols 1 and 2; *Crossing Subject Boundaries; Some Routes through the Guides.*)

The guides provide a very thorough discussion of topics. As well as including material which would be directly relevant to pupils, they provide teachers with a valuable background which will deepen their understanding and give them insight into mathematical thinking. At many points, it is made clear that some of the material discussed may not enter into the course of work which pupils will follow.

With the publication of the first guides in 1970, Philip Floyd felt that the onus for implementation had passed to the local education authorities. They must use the guides to follow courses of action suited to the local need.

Comments from schools

While a study of the guides would undoubtedly help to develop an understanding of mathematics, many comments from schools indicated that they have been of only limited value to teachers whose own mathematical knowledge was slight – many teachers have found them difficult to assimilate. They acknowledged that the ideas were good, but several comments received suggested that few teachers would have the time and energy to draw out the teaching points, construct the necessary workbooks and worksheets, and to type and duplicate them themselves as in general they have to. (The need for clerical support in curriculum development in schools is indicated.) As one school commented:

> The lack of pupil material has involved the teachers in a lot of preparation of work cards, worksheets and other modes of assignments and this has, understandably, reduced the amount of work attempted and progress has been slow.

Nevertheless, we received some very positive comments from some schools:

> . . . used the material with the lower ability range in the fourth year. We were quite pleased with the results. I was quite startled by the change in attitude. They were much more interested than in previous years and attendance noticeably improved. One group were, in fact, often early in their arrival at Maths lessons! This had not happened before in my nine years of teaching. They took work home to be completed and we had some very colourful and interesting wall-displays.

This teacher sent in examples of worksheets. He had found *Luck and Judgement* fruitful; but he had also produced a whole series on linkage, which incorporated

132

good quality photographic reproduction in duplicated material. Using Meccano, he had worked out activities and produced worksheets to assist the pupils in learning about quadrilateral linkage, parallelogram linkage, a rhombic linkage and variable base linkages.

A Burnley teacher wrote: 'On the whole I would say that this new approach has been highly satifactory with this particular type of boy.' He had in mind a group of forty-eight fourth-year boys, 'some of whom had been promoted from a remedial class, some of them have by virtue of ability naturally found themselves in this class and some of them have rejected all forms of orthodox education.' He had had good results using Mathematics for the Majority with topics such as: shapes; rotary to linear motion; basic time study; number patterns; curve-stitching; gears; model-making.

We also observed a class of 13-year-olds deeply absorbed in activities derived from the teachers' guide, *Luck and Judgement*. They were spinning coins and shaking beads in a variety of containers, and the atmosphere of activity had much in common with that of a good primary school. The pupils were interested and enthusiastic: 'It is better than ordinary maths,' one said. The main reservation expressed by the teacher was that progress was very slow – not much was seen to be done. He felt that this was more than compensated for by 'the quality of learning'. The only other guide which he felt was likely to be much help was *From Counting to Calculating*. This young teacher had prepared a large number of worksheets and had carefully planned his lessons, so that the classroom scene was very rewarding to witness.

Summary

Although the guides were considered by many teachers to be difficult reading, they do constitute a valuable source of background ideas about mathematics in relation to many topics which are part of most people's everyday experience. The interested teacher, determined enough to fill in his own background knowledge and understanding, would undoubtedly gain from this. To some degree at least it would be essential in order to make the best use of the many suggestions for classroom work to stimulate and interest less successful pupils. There would, however, be the further problem, particularly with the disadvantaged, of preparing suitable workcards and workbooks. This problem has been taken up by the Continuation Project.

Mathematics for the Majority Continuation Project

Whereas Mathematics for the Majority had concentrated on producing teachers' guides, the Continuation Project was firmly committed to producing pupil material. Its aims were defined as:

1. develop pupil assignments and study guides related to the Mathematics for the Majority teachers' guides, other published texts, and new packs of source materials including film loops, audio-tapes and pictorial material developed simultaneously by the project team;
2. maintain contact with the network of associated schools already built up by the Mathematics for the Majority Project by testing different parts of the new materials in different groups of the schools, and by inviting local groups of teachers to contribute to the development of the new materials, especially the individual assignments;
3. produce one further teachers' guide to the new pupil material.

An elaborate system of writing groups and regional co-ordinators has been established to ensure that the materials originate with experienced teachers. The strong editorial team then prepare this material for publication. The teachers are being encouraged to think in multi-media terms – work cards, photographs, tapes, films and loops, models and basic apparatus, games and puzzles, were all mentioned. A list of topics for the writing groups has been circulated through the project's magazine *Newsmaths* – for example, mathematics and aircraft, mathematics in athletics, mathematics of buildings, mathematics in the factory, mathematics and fashion, mathematics and holidays, etc.

It was possible to examine in trial form the kits 'Communications' and 'Living in Cities', and to visit schools using them. The Continuation Project has produced lively and varied materials. 'Communications' is presented in a strong box containing a teacher's manual, a tape cassette, a map, and more than fifty work cards and information sheets on many topics allied to communication. The topics include: newspapers; words and letters; the telephone; television; circuits; routes; home and abroad; letters, paper and envelopes; traffic in towns; one-way system; the Underground; travel to school; postage.

Schools have reported encouragingly about work of this kind, often referring to such benefits as an increase in keenness to learn, in inventiveness and, in the case of one practical topic, in manual dexterity.

It is a frequent comment of teachers that project materials and ideas have aroused a high level of interest, but they are uncertain about how to ensure progress in concepts and skills. One school pointed out that project work took only two-fifths of the available mathematics time, and an attempt was made to arrange for the skills likely to be needed in topics to be acquired more systematically in other periods. Curiosity and interest, however, beget learning and there can be no doubt that the production of thematic learning materials is to be welcomed. The methods adopted by the Continuation Project provide for the maximum of teacher participation, and the editorial team has the resources to bring all this material into focus. Teachers of disadvantaged children will be well advised to keep track of the work done at Exeter.

The materials are being published by Schofield & Sims.

Concluding discussion

A first problem in planning mathematics courses for disadvantaged children is to decide what the aims and objectives should be. Philip Floyd has referred to these pupils as 'floating in a mathematical limbo'. On the one hand there are pupils taking courses leading to examinations and on the other hand those who need remedial teaching. Mathematics teachers have tended to be uncertain about the content and methods of courses for non-examination pupils while remedial teachers working with the weakest pupils have tended to be preoccupied with basic computational skills and with social arithmetic.

Unfortunately, very little has been written about the teaching of mathematics to slower children in secondary schools. At the remedial level, little has been published since Fred J. Schonell's *Diagnosis and Remedial Teaching in Arithmetic*, published by Oliver & Boyd in 1957. There are only a few textbooks specifically written for slow learners. Compared with the output of articles on various aspects of teaching English and reading to slow learners in secondary schools, there is a dearth of articles on mathematics which probably reflects a lack of experiment and discussion.

It seems desirable to state some of the issues which the teacher should consider even if it would be difficult to make a definitive statement of aims. A first issue is what importance should be given to the acquisition of computational skills. In the introduction to the teachers' guide *From Counting to Calculating*, it is suggested that pupils, parents, employers and most teachers rate arithmetic highly mainly because it is considered useful in everyday life and in many jobs. The authors go on to say, however, that computation is often overrated and this can lead to unnecessary emphasis on the acquisition of skill in many arithmetical techniques. Chapter 1 of *From Counting to Calculating* reports the views of teachers on what number facts and what mental and written computational skills should be achieved by a 16-year-old school leaver not sitting a CSE examination. A wide range of opinion, especially for mental and written computation, was revealed but the items generally supported would provide a useful starting point for discussion within a school or in groups at teachers' centres.

Content is important, but so is the question of how these computational skills should be acquired. Schools Council projects provide a wide range of ideas on how these basic concepts and skills can be taught in ways which avoid the dreary dullness of much former mathematics teaching with slow learners. With children in the younger age groups, there would be value in secondary teachers making themselves acquainted with the methods of modern primary mathematics. With older pupils, useful suggestions are made in the Mathematics for the Majority Project's *From Counting to Calculating* and *Number Appreciation* and the Midland Mathematics Experiment's *Excursions from Mathematics*. As pupils come nearer to leaving school, there is often a stronger motivation to improve basic skills which can be the cue for a further attempt at remedial work and also for practising skills in topics related to everyday needs and interests in post-school life.

The need for assessment and diagnostic work is one which has not received much attention, although the wide range of attainment requires grouping or setting to ensure that pupils are being given work suited to their level and to their weaknesses. The lack of appropriate tests is a common complaint of teachers, especially of remedial teachers. Some of the long-established tests are out of date and not appropriate to modern mathematics learning. Other mathematics tests designed to assess attainment over the ability range have limited value for diagnostic purposes and may be difficult to apply with slow learners. A solution might be found in the concept of 'criterion-referenced' tests rather than 'norm-referenced' tests. That is, having decided what basic mathematical concepts and skills are aimed for at any age or class level, items can be constructed to test whether they have, in fact, been acquired. One is not concerned here with standardization and norms since comparisons are not being made with other pupils. The information sought is simply whether the pupil knows certain facts, understands certain concepts, or can undertake certain calculations. The procedure is similar to that in programmed learning in which, when learning has not taken place to some criterion level, revision or a remedial activity is provided.

A second issue is what importance should be given to any mathematics which may be required for 'social competence'? Teachers of slow learners have a particular concern to ensure that pupils whose adjustment to working and social life may be rather precarious are aware of, and have thought about, such topics as budgeting, hire-purchase, savings, income tax, insurance and other deductions from wages, the costs of clothes, food, holidays and leisure activities. In addition, particular attention is paid to money (giving and receiving change) and to concepts of time and their application to everyday situations. Commonly, these form

136

part of the preparation for leaving school in special schools. These basic ideas are needed not only by very slow learners but also by other pupils from disadvantaged backgrounds. This is not necessarily a job for the mathematics teacher. It may find a place in several areas of the curriculum – for example, in social studies and home economics. It is represented in the Mathematics for the Majority Project and in the Continuation Project.

A third issue is that mathematics should be viewed as an important means of improving thinking and the use of language – two important aspects of compensatory education for the disadvantaged. A selection of mathematical topics and activities can be made which enable pupils to think and talk about mathematical relationships and to appreciate in some measure the order and pattern of their environment. Since less successful pupils are more at home with familiar experience, it is useful to emphasize applications of mathematics in the community, in science and in many everyday situations (e.g. sport, newspapers, transport). Selection will depend on the ability, experience and interest of pupils although, as examples in this chapter show, successful and enjoyable work can take place with pupils who start from a very limited position.

A final issue is that the mathematics undertaken should give enjoyment and satisfaction. It is clear that some of the activities suggested by the projects have this desirable result, and often counteract negative attitudes. We have observed numerous examples of pupils working at mathematics with enthusiasm and enjoyment. There is no doubt at all that mathematics can be made an exciting, absorbing experience even to very backward pupils, but success in mathematics depends more upon the enthusiasm of the teacher than perhaps in any other area of the curriculum. The teachers who were succeeding seemed to have in common the fact that they were enjoying the exploration of new approaches themselves. The publications of the various mathematics projects are a useful source of ideas and guidance for developing more varied work with slow learners and disadvantaged children, and avoiding too great a restriction in the content and methods of mathematics teaching.

IX. Design and craft education

Disadvantaged children are often able to achieve normally and to experience satisfaction and a measure of success in some aspect of practical or creative work. In some cases, craft has been related to education for leisure, or to home economics or it has had a community service purpose (such as making toys for playgroups). In some schools, particularly in special schools for slow learners, large-scale projects, perhaps involving building or construction, have been found valuable. Pupils enjoy the practical activity and the sense of doing a 'real job'. They gain in knowledge and skill as well as benefiting from the experience of carrying a job through. It is not uncommon for some of the least likely pupils to show unsuspected qualities of co-operation, persistence and initiative.

Teachers who are attracted to this kind of approach would be interested in the ideas and the experience of the Design and Craft Project which, by its emphasis on pupils' identification of a problem, and the need to design a solution and evaluate it, has suggested ways in which this kind of work can be effectively taken a stage further.

A feasibility study based at the University of Leicester produced Schools Council Working Paper 26: *Education through the Use of Materials: the Possible Role of School Workshops in the Education of Secondary-school Pupils* (Evans/Methuen Educational, 1969). This was a very forward-looking document, and argued that handicraft teachers, through their technical skills and knowledge and the resources at their disposal, are in a strong position to assist their pupils to develop 'not only motor skills and craftsmanship, but also many intellectual qualities that hitherto have been associated mainly with other subject areas.'

Areas of possible development were suggested under the headings of: design; preparation for occupational role; community service projects; school service projects; recreational equipment projects; and foundation courses.

Perhaps the most interesting of these were the proposals for community service projects. After warning of the difficulty of organizing such projects because this often requires an excessive amount of time, the working paper points out that such projects may contribute to the more general aspects of handicraft – for example, the processes of planning and design, the selection and use of tools and the expansion of technical knowledge can go hand in hand with the achievement of social objectives. Flexibility of timetable and personnel would seem to be essential. It was also felt that such activities, though demanding, should not

138

be limited to parts of the school year when the serious work of examinations was finished. 'Community service is, indeed, applicable to no one age or ability group and may be a continuous part of education.' One northern school undertook to produce toys for the local day nursery. The task was undertaken as an on-going part of their craft lessons and was left entirely in the hands of a group of fourth-formers who arranged a visit to the nursery in order to discuss the project, and designed and produced the toys.

School service projects are similar, but related only to the immediate school environment. Large ventures undoubtedly catch the imagination of pupils and many, such as major building projects, have illustrated that pupils of low academic ability can be engaged in productive activity, even where the end-product will be of little benefit to themselves since they will have left the school before the project is complete, and that they will participate in such work with an eagerness not always associated with the majority of C and D stream pupils in the normal work environment.

With the stimulating ideas of this working paper as its basis, the Design and Craft Education Project was set up at the University of Keele under the direction of Professor S. John Eggleston, with A. R. Pemberton and D. Taberner as research fellows. The project materials are being published by Edward Arnold. The work was in five main areas:

1 *Materials, discovery and design.* The development of the design process, upon which this section is based, is fundamental to the project's thinking. Thus, given a problem, such as the need of a disabled person for a simple piece of equipment that will enable him to perform a particular action, students are encouraged to identify and specify the problem (e.g. what the equipment is for, what materials are advisable), accept the restraints, engage in pre-design and research discussion with other students and teachers, produce models in card, clay, etc., consolidate workable solutions into controlled areas of manufacture, discuss and modify, produce a solution and finally assess its success.

2 *Materials and domestic life.* Here the pupil is working not only with wood, but with a whole range of materials from plastics to new decorating materials. Work undertaken may include conversion, renovation and maintenance of the home, interior and exterior decoration, layout of gardens, minor building projects and appreciation of household equipment. The whole field of consumer expertise is an integral part of this work and again a problem-solving approach is adopted.

3 *Materials and community development.* Pupils are encouraged to identify school and community needs, translate these into design terms, formulate

139

proposals and implement these under staff guidance. Projects undertaken in the trial schools included working with geriatric patients, preparing play equipment in educational priority areas and helping to restore parts of Fountains Abbey.

4 *Materials and work.* In association with colleges of further education, attempts are being made to explore the implications of link courses. Production-line situations in the school workshop are being developed for short-term adoption to include concepts such as cost-benefit analysis, quantity and variation and labour intensity. Besides school-based 'factory day' approaches, the project was also interested in developing schemes of 'work experience'.

5 *Materials and leisure.* Included in this section are suggestions for ways in which leisure time can be used, ranging from toy- and model-making, through photography, karting and land yachts to the theatre.

It might seem that there is little need to argue the case for practical subjects, since these activities are very popular among school leavers and their parents. Two reservations have to be made, however. First, RoSLA pupils and their parents take a much more pragmatic view of these subjects than do most teachers – the latter stress educational and ethical values, the former are mainly concerned with vocational aspects. There is the possibility of a clash, or at least a major difference in emphasis, between the teachers and pupils. Secondly, we should not fall into the trap of assuming that all disadvantaged pupils have an aptitude for practical work. Many will be as weak in these subjects as they are in others, or weaker.

Many of the projects inspired by the Design and Craft Project team have provided opportunities for the less competent boys and girls to contribute something to the final product. These activities seem particularly important, since the feeling of being excluded from school activities is an important component in producing alienation among adolescents.

Issues of *Survey*, an occasional publication of the Design and Craft Project, have contained interesting accounts from trial schools of activities in which disadvantaged children were involved. Since these illustrate well the project's approach and the value of such activities for disadvantaged children, we base the remainder of this chapter, with the project team's permission, on these accounts.

One report, written under the title 'Young hooligans and school projects' describes how some of the most difficult boys in a secondary modern school in Cheshire became involved in a community service project. A member of the central team introduced the idea to the boys. He explained that children suffering from a congenital defect were often unable to walk. They could only stand with some support and some of the children had their legs in plaster, so that when they sat they had to have their legs splayed out straight and horizontal. Some sort of trolley might give such a child independence and relieve the mother very greatly. The boys were immediately keen, although this involved them in considerable extra work. 'Limbs of young children would have to be measured and their contours moulded in plaster. Sketches would have to be made, and prototypes knocked up. This might not all be done between 9.0 a.m. and 4.0 p.m. at school. A method of mass production would have to be thought out if a number of vehicles were to be produced in a given time. Would the lads work "factory hours" at least from 8.30 a.m. to 5.0 p.m. on two consecutive days? Would they put in overtime to complete the work if necessary, all unpaid? No doubt about it, they certainly would!'

It required considerable ingenuity to make the timetable flexible enough for the young designers and production planners to meet, discuss and decide upon the ideas to be accepted. Eventually, the designs were chosen and broken down into individual or group operations, and preparations were made for the factory days.

Trolleys and walkers were completed by boys and teachers working overtime on both factory days and other days as well. The completed trolleys were delivered to the local medical institute for trials and evaluation and eventually presented to local spina bifida children, while other equipment was delivered to an orthopaedic hospital.

The headmaster of the school where this work was carried out then volunteered some reflections on the boys who had so promptly and willingly given their services:

As I read the names I realized that a number of the boys had appeared before different juvenile courts recently. Two, for instance, had been involved, with others, one evening in smashing a sports shop window and making off with whatever they could grab quickly. They had no use for the articles they took but threw them away. Yet another three had stolen sheath knives during the school holidays, and used them to threaten girls. Serious charges had been made but the boys had claimed it was 'just a giggle'. Six other boys had been in trouble with the police over fighting at a Fourth Division football match. They also minimized the seriousness of their offence.

It dawned on me with surprise that at least a half of the 'Factory Days' volunteers had been involved in acts of hooliganism about the town, and that I had written reports on them for juvenile courts. There was substantial uniformity about the reports. I could not say that any one of them was openly aggressive or unpleasant in school. They were somehow 'unorganizable', though forming a clearly distinguishable 'sub-group' within their year group. They were the boys who could never bother to bring swimming trunks for baths mornings, or PE kit for games days.

This concept of the 'factory day' linked to a community project seemed to us imaginative and to be offering a real opportunity to break through the crust of indifference and rejection that so many young school leavers have developed.

> The 'Factory Days' cut right through the normal timetable, and the disruption made the whole school, particularly young staff, aware of the project. It caught the imagination of those boys most closely involved, and took them on a spiritual adventure such as comes infrequently to us in our lifetime. It was not something pushed to produce house points, but was, as the boys said, 'dead serious'. There was no promise of reward. This project was offered as a yoke, in the same shape almost as the 'blood, toil, tears and sweat' of Garibaldi and Churchill.
> The young 'hooligans' accepted this yoke readily, and found it easy, and naturally borne. Had it been presented in any other way it might have been mistaken for a fetter. And youth today is not inclined to wear chains – other than those it chooses for decoration.

An internal project was carried out at a school in the West Riding, in which the pupils built a garage in the school grounds. The teacher recorded with due modesty 'a quite professional standard was achieved by boys of 13 to 15 years, on a total budget of £80'. He found that visitors often queried whether all the work was done by the boys and the answer is 'Yes, easily.' For example, they dug the 11 ft × 4 ft 6 in × 4 ft inspection pit out of hard shale in their dinner-break as a bit of fun.

It seems that planning and drawing represent the most difficult part of any such operation, though to the amateur do-it-yourself handyman the illustration of the finished product is a little awe-inspiring.

Another project undertaken was land yachting in a Yorkshire school. The first difficulty in this project arose over timetables and workshop space. This was overcome by making the woodwork and metalwork rooms available one after-noon a week. It was understood that the success or failure of the project would depend entirely on the reactions of the pupils themselves. Owing to lack of in-formation and visual aids of any kind, the idea of a land yacht was shelved and pupils were asked to design and build a vehicle with which they were familiar – a trolley.

When the trolleys were constructed, enthusiasm waned as the pupils ran out of energy pushing the trolleys up and down, and a lively discussion ensued about

142

means of motivation. Someone suggested a sail and unwittingly launched the project.

Pupils organized themselves into work teams, each team having an expert in charge. In conjunction with the PE department, a dinghy kit had been purchased for the girls to build. It soon became apparent that some girls wished to work on the land yacht and some boys on the dinghy. Many were the looks of amazement from members of staff as they passed the workshops and saw the odd assembly of tubes, wheels and valuable scrap. Questions such as 'What time did you finish last night?' or 'You were here early this morning!' indicated the pupils' enthusiasm.

A pair of alloy wheels appeared, a gift from one of the parents, many parents were becoming as interested as their sons and daughters.

At last, the wheels and steering were completed and the mast and sail from the dinghy were commissioned as a temporary measure. One week later, the land yacht was assembled in the school playground. No shortage of volunteer 'test pilots' was encountered but the results were unsatisfactory and it was soon discovered that the mast was too far forward. This was rectified and the results were amazing. Since its trial the land yacht has been used extensively by the pupils.

The biggest changes noticed as a result of this project were on the social side. Boys and girls accepted each other working as a team and the barrier between teacher and pupil soon disappeared.

'In a narrow sense this project did provide the answer to the problem of meeting the needs of the fourth-year non-certificate pupil.' It was found to be so successful that even before completion the vital work of planning the next project was under consideration. It was hoped that it too, like the land yacht, would go 'like the clappers'.

Appendices

Appendix A   Report on the use of Schools Council Moral Education Curriculum Project material (*Lifeline*) with slow learners in a comprehensive school

The material made available to the school was: *Sensitivity, Consequences, Points of View*, and this was used once or twice a week with fourth-year pupils from March to July 1972. These youngsters were the least able in the school. A small group of fifth-year pupils also used some of the material (*Points of View*) as a post-CSE examination activity.

Role-playing proved too difficult for the fourth-year pupils (more a reflection perhaps of the teaching they had received than of the material), but they readily discussed and wrote about various situations.

Consequences perhaps gave the most successful results. The following are examples of the suggestions attempted in the trial materials, and some of the writing stimulated by them is given below:

> Outline what would happen if someone took an electric fire into the bathroom.
> What would happen if someone emptied oil waste into a lake?
> What would happen if someone placed a concrete block on a railway line?
> Outline what would happen if someone allowed a dog out on its own.
> What might happen if someone locked a 6-year-old child outside from 2–10 at night?

Some topics from the *Points of View* material were concerned with age conflicts between grandparent and grandchild living under the same roof and psychological problems, stammering, etc.

Some amendments to suit the local group of children were introduced (e.g. in the second suggestion listed the place became a local park, and in the fourth the dog became an Alsatian because one of the group owned a particularly ferocious specimen).

Material used from the three booklets made available was chosen for its possible familiarity to the pupils. At least one member's contribution would be enlightened by experience.

145

The oral part of the lessons was inevitably fuller than these written comments and stories show. Without exception, all the pupils could contribute usefully in the lengthy discussions, which sometimes produced very valuable 'red herrings'. For example, the last suggestion about the child being locked out of the house raised the actual situation of a child 6 years old being locked out of his home (or any shelter) for up to eight hours at a time.

It is interesting to note that several of the situations triggered off part-fantasy stories from some of the girls. (They were encouraged to write like this if they preferred.)

All this material is a very useful contribution to real teaching situations with slower pupils, and provides a collection of ideas for teachers to adapt to their own children's needs. There will be fuller use of the material in the remedial department with a wider age range in future.

Consequences

Oil in the lake

Child K. Non-verbal IQ 86*
Could kill the fish and for people who do fishing. The oil could get into the fish and people going fishing could eat the fish and then could die.

Child P. Non-verbal IQ 78
1   It would kill off the fish.
2   It smells and it stops people fishing.
3   Spoils boys swimming and camping there.
4   Blocks up mains and you have dirty drinking water.
5   Dirties water-birds' feathers and kills them when they try to clean themselves.
6   Kills insects which are food for birds. Kills flowers and grass.
7   How did the oil get there?
8   It might have got there by someone cleaning the waste oil out the car.

Child Kl. Non-verbal IQ 83
1   It might kill off any fish.
2   It might make a terrible smell.
3   Someone else might get blamed for it.
4   The one that done it might run away.
5   Someone might have just emptied waste oil out of the car without knowing what might happen.

   * The non-verbal IQ scores throughout were obtained by the pupils in the fourth year of the junior school on NFER Primary Non-verbal Test 3.

Fire in the bathroom

Child Kl. Non-verbal IQ 83

1   The person in the bath might get over-heated.
2   He might splash the heater and ruin it.
3   It might start a fire, and it might affect something else in the house.
4   He might rush to turn the heater off and burn himself badly.
5   He might try to escape out the window. He could get hurt. The fire might blaze up even more.

Concrete block on a railway line

Child L. Non-verbal IQ 80

If concrete blocks was on a train line. The train could crash. People could get killed. The train could stop in time and a train coming the same way would run into it. The train would hit the electric wire.

Child J. Non-verbal IQ 81

1   *The train.* The train would probably crash and explode. There could be another train behind the train. They then would have to stop.
2   *The people.* The people would probably be shocked and they might panic. Some of the people could be killed of this concrete. It might be too late to save the people.
3   *The person who put the concrete there.* The person who put the concrete would probably put it there for a laugh. He might want to rob the train. He could be caught and taken to court. For having put the concrete there for some people might be killed for having put the concrete there.

Alsatian loose in the road

Child L. Non-verbal IQ 80

If you let a dog go out on its own, it could get losted. Go in someone's home or garden. Get someone's leg. Go for the farmer's cows. Go on the train line and the train could get knocked over on the lines and make a mess.

Child Ja. Non-verbal IQ 84

If someone lets a alsatian run free it might bite people and it might get killed. When all the cars come on the road, or the people have been to work or wherever they have been. If the alsatian dog did get killed the persons whose car killed the alsatian dog would feel responsible. The person would probably stop the car, lots of people would stare at them. They would get the dog in the car and take them to the vet. The person would tell the vet what happened. The vet will say to the man I will keep and bury him. The man will go and tell the police. The police will try and find the owner of the dog. If they cannot find the owner of the alsatian dog they will put it into the paper or in the shop window. If they don't have the paper or go in the shop or if they don't go and look in the shop window they will then just leave it and till they do find out.

Child Kh. Non-verbal IQ 79

There was an alsatian loose in the street. There was a car going 50 mph. The alsatian ran out. The man who was driving had his family in the back. He swerved off the dog and there was another car on the other side of the road where it was parked. He hit it and he killed two of his family. The dog was running loose. It had no collar or no name disc. When they caught the dog they had to put it to sleep because they did not know whose dog it was. They could not find them.

Consequences: Two people killed. Two cars smashed. The driver would feel rotten because two of his family were dead. The driver was cut and bruised. The dog lost its life. The ambulance men had a nasty job.

Locked out

Child P. Non-verbal IQ 78

1   The child would probably go hungry and start bothering neighbours for food.
2   He could cut himself and have nowhere to go.
3   The child could wander off looking for his grandad and get lost or taken away.
4   There would be no shelter, no conveniences for the child to use.
5   The child might try to climb into the house and get hurt. He might fall from a high window or cut himself on a broken window.
6   He might ask strangers to get him into the house.
7   If he got in there are dangers indoors for a 6-year-old: gas, electricity, cooking.

Points of view

Child lost in a shopping complex

Child D. Non-verbal I Q 73

Mrs Smith and her daughter went shopping on a Saturday afternoon. They got off the bus and walked to the shopping centre. Mrs Smith and her daughter Jane went in the record shop first to buy a record and then they went in Tesco's to get some food. Mrs Smith was talking to a friend. Jane was looking for some sweets around the corner from where her mother was talking, there's a lot of counters and bends in Tesco's, and when she turned round one of the bends and her mother was gone. Jane walked right down to the bottom of the shop. She still couldn't find her mother, and she started to cry and panic and she started to run round the shop, scared and frightened. But suddenly she heard a voice and it was saying – Jane Smith, aged 4, long blond hair. Please come to the toy counter. Jane stopped suddenly and in front of her was her mother standing by the toys. Mrs Smith ran to her daughter Jane. Jane started to cry and her mother did. When they'd calmed down a bit, they went on with the rest of the shopping. Mrs Smith made sure that she held on to Jane's hand.

Child Ja. Non-verbal I Q 84

Jane would feel very upset when she saw she was lost she might cry hoping that her mom would come. When her mom comes out of the shop and finds that Jane is missing she would be upset. She might think that somebody took her. Jane's mom would then go to the nearest police station and tell them what has happened. They would then tell two policemen to get the car and look for a girl, aged 5. If they find her the lady will be very pleased and she would say thank you to the policemen for finding my little girl. The girl would still be crying a bit then she would stop and be pleased. She would say to her mom – I will hold your hand all the time now because I do not want to get lost again, I have had enough for one day.

Age conflicts

Child W. Non-verbal I Q 81

I would give a sound-proof room for gran as she does not like loud music and Ann does. It would not be fair if gran said she could not have any music on. I would also give Ann some earphones so that gran would not be able to hear the music that is on. And I would also let Ann play music on certain days when gran

149

has gone out that would then be fair for gran and Ann. It would be also fair if Ann goes to her friend's house some days while gran then can do what she wants to. Ann's friend then can come to Ann's house while gran is out. I don't think it would be fair if Ann gave gran some drugs or an earplug because gran would not do that to Ann so I don't think I would have the drugs. I might give her earplugs if she wanted them or otherwise I would not give her earplugs.

Child Pd. Non-verbal I Q 86

Ann likes pop music loud and gran moans.

1 Soundproof room.
2 Give gran half the house.
3 Stop Ann's music.
4 Make Ann wear earphones.
5 Ann only play her discs on certain days or when gran is out.
5a Ann go to her friend's house some days and her friend come to Ann's on other days.
6 Drug gran or give her earplugs.

I would choose 5a because it will be better for gran some day and Ann's friend's mother. More convenient for Ann and gran. So if gran don't like the situation tell her to write and tell us at our school address and we will make further inquiries into the matter.

Age conflicts – 'The good old days'

Child W. Non-verbal I Q 81

Clare is 15. How would she feel when gran told her about when she was that age. Clare would feel rather bored when she criticized the younger generation of today, thoughts passing through Clare's head:

> 'Oh, why doesn't she shut up?'
> 'She's off again.'
> 'I think she must think it's as what she calls the "golden" days before the war.'

What would make her feel better was when gran told her about the pranks that she used to get up to.

Child S. Non-verbal IQ 76

Clare's gran was talking about the olden days and Clare was so bored that she kept on doing odd jobs for her mother. But Clare kept telling her gran that was different in them days. Gran kept telling Clare that the clothes we wore could not be minis, they had to be below our knees and the make-up we wore could be only lipstick, not eye shadow like today. And if we wanted to go out we had to tell our father where we was going and who we was with and what time you be back and if we was not back on the proper time we told him he used to be on the doorstep waiting for me to come.

Child J. Non-verbal IQ 81

Clare would feel bored after listening to gran and also be amused at what gran says. The sort of things that gran would talk about would be the style of hair, and what time you would have to be in when she was a child. Also the sort of fashion you would wear and you would not wear make-up until you were 16 years old.

Psychological problems

An elderly man comes into the employment exchange. He starts to speak:
'I w–w–w–w–w– a–a–a–a– nt –t–t–t–'
'Take it easy dad and get it out' said the clerk.

1   What do you think of the clerk's attitude?
2   What do you think it is like to stammer?

Child Ja. Non-verbal IQ 84

I think when the clerk said take it easy and get it out I thought it was very kind of the clerk. Because some people who are clerks are not very kind to people who cannot get the words out. The people who are not kind to people who cannot get the words out right. They take the mickey out of them and they feel embarrassed as they are taking the mickey out of them.
To be a stammer – it would not be very nice as people will stare at you and you would feel embarrassed. Some people who are not so kind might start to laugh at you and you might feel upset as they are laughing at you as you cannot get all the words out that you want to. And people who stammer might have an important message and cannot get it out and the person might say leave it. If a

151

person who is not so kind knows anyone who is a stammer, he might stop away from that person as they cannot understand what they are saying.

Appendix B Publications and materials from projects referred to

Full details should be obtained from the publishers of each project's materials. Materials published since this survey are marked with an asterisk.

Schools Council projects
Scope (English for Immigrant Children Project)
Publisher: Longman, Longman House, Burnt Mill, Harlow, Essex
Scope Stage 1
Scope Stage 2
Scope Senior Course
*Talking in Class and **Scope 1* (films). Hire or purchase from National Audio-Visual Aids Library, Paxton Place, Gipsy Road, London SE27 9SR.

Concept 7–9 (Teaching English to West Indian Children Project)
Publisher: E. J. Arnold, Butterley Street, Leeds LS10 1AX
Unit 1 *Listening with Understanding*   Unit 3 *Communication*
Unit 2 *Concept Building*   Unit 4 *The Dialect Kit*
*Concept 7–9 (film). Hire or purchase from NAVAL.
(The units are published in the US as *Concepts for Communication* by Developmental Learning Materials, Illinois.)

Social Education Project
No teaching materials.
*The report of the project is published as Schools Council Working Paper 51, *Social Education: an Experiment in Four Secondary Schools* (Evans/Methuen Educational).

Integrated Studies
Publisher: Oxford University Press, Education Department, Walton Street, Oxford OX2 6DP
**Unit 1 *Exploration Man*   Unit 2 *Communicating with Others*

152

Unit 3   *Living Together*   *Unit 4   *Groups in Society*
Exploration Man: an Introduction to Integrated Studies (for teachers)
Teachers' Guide (Units 2 and 3)

Geography for the Young School Leaver
Publisher: Thomas Nelson & Sons, 36 Park Street, London W1Y 4DE
Only trial material was available at the time of the survey.
*Theme 1   *Man, Land and Leisure*
*Theme 2   *Cities and People*
*Theme 3   *People, Place and Work*

Lifeline (*Moral Education Curriculum Project*)
Publisher: Longman
In Other People's Shoes (Three sets of cards and one teacher's book)
   Sensitivity, Consequences, Points of View
Proving the Rule? (Five short books)
What would you have done? (Six short books and slides. Slides available from
Slide Centre Ltd, Portman House, 17 Brodrick Road, London SW17 7DZ.)
For teachers:
Moral Education in the Secondary School
Our School

Religious Education in Secondary Schools
Publisher: Hart-Davis Educational, Granada Publishing, Frogmore, St Albans,
Herts
Publication of thirty packs of pupils' and teachers' materials will begin in 1975.

Science 5–13
Publisher: Macdonald Educational, 49/50 Poland Street, London W1A 2LG
Teachers' Units:

With Objectives in Mind	*Structures and Forces* Stages 1 and 2
Early Experiences	*Structures and Forces* Stage 3
Working with Wood Stages 1 and 2	*Change* Stages 1 and 2, and background
Working with Wood Background	
Time Stages 1 and 2, and background	*Change* Stage 3
	Minibeasts Stages 1 and 2
Science from Toys Stages 1 and 2, and background	*Holes, Gaps and Cavities* Stages 1 and 2

Metals Stages 1 and 2
Metals Background
Ourselves Stages 1 and 2
Like and Unlike Stages 1, 2 and 3
Children and Plastics Stages 1 and 2, and background
Coloured Things Stages 1 and 2

Science, Models and Toys Stage 3
Trees Stages 1 and 2
Using the Environment
 1. *Early Explorations*
 2. *Investigations* Parts 1 and 2
 3. *Tackling Problems* Parts 1 and 2
 4. *Ways and Means*

Mathematics for the Majority
Publisher: Chatto & Windus Educational, Granada Publishing, Frogmore, St Albans, Herts
Teachers' guides:

Mathematical Experience
Machines, Mechanisms and Mathematics
Assignment Systems
Luck and Judgement
Mathematical Pattern
Number Appreciation
Mathematics from Outdoors

From Counting to Calculating
Some Simple Functions
Algebra of a Sort
Geometry for Enjoyment
Space Travel and Mathematics, Vols 1 and 2
Crossing Subject Boundaries
Some Routes through the Guides

Mathematics for the Majority Continuation Project
Publisher: Schofield & Sims, 35 St John's Road, Huddersfield, HD1 5DT
Packs of pupils' materials; each pack has its own teacher's handbook.
Buildings
Communication
Countryside
Family

Motor Car
Physical Recreation
Seas and Rivers
Travel

Design and Craft
Publisher: Edward Arnold, 25 Hill Street, London W1X 8LL
Books for teachers and pupils, with filmstrips:
Materials and Design: a Fresh Approach
Design for Today (with five filmstrips)
You are a Designer
Education through Design and Craft
Connections and Constructions
Nine filmstrips on design principles
Design with a Purpose (film). Hire or purchase from NAVAL.

154

Schools Council/Nuffield projects

Breakthrough to Literacy (Initial Literacy Project)
Publisher: Longman, Longman House, Burnt Mill, Harlow, Essex
Teacher's Manual
Teacher's Sentence Maker   *My First Word Book
My Sentence Maker   *Second Word Maker
First Word Maker
Breakthrough Books (*Several have been published since the end of the survey – notably the Green Set readers which are especially designed for older, less-able children.)
(*Breakthrough to Literacy* is published in the US by Bowmar Publishing, Glendale, California.)

Language in Use Project
Publisher: Edward Arnold   *Work with Language
Language in Use   *Using Language in Use
Exploring Language   (These two titles, produced after the
Language, 'English' and the Curriculum   project ended, are published by
Language in Use tape   Edward Arnold as follow-up material
                                         for teachers.)

Humanities Curriculum Project
Publisher: Heinemann Educational Books, 48 Charles Street, London W1X 8AH
The Humanities Project: an Introduction
Collections of material on the following themes:
War and society   People and work
Education   Poverty
The family   Law and order
Relations between the sexes   Living in cities

Nuffield projects

Nuffield Junior Science
Publisher: William Collins, Sons & Co., 14 St James's Place, London SW1
Teacher's Guide 1   Teacher's background booklets:
Teacher's Guide 2   *Autumn into Winter*
Source books: *Science and History*
Apparatus   *Mammals in Classrooms*
Animals and Plants

Nuffield Combined Science
Publisher: Penguin Education, and Longman Group, Pinnacles, Harlow, Essex

Teacher's Guide I	*Activities Pack I* ⎫
Teacher's Guide II	*Activities Pack II* ⎬ Comprising ten booklets
Teacher's Guide III	⎭

Nuffield Secondary Science
Publisher: Longman Group
Teachers' Guide

Theme 1 *Interdependence of Living Things*

Theme 2 *Continuity of Life*

Theme 3 *Biology of Man*

Theme 4 *Harnessing Energy*

Theme 5 *Extension of Sense Perception*

Theme 6 *Movement*

Theme 7 *Using Materials*

Theme 8 *The Earth and Its Place in the Universe*

Apparatus Guide
Background books for pupils:
*Britain's Fuels
*Rocks, Minerals and Fossils

Nuffield Mathematics Project
Publisher: W. & R. Chambers, 11 Thistle Street, Edinburgh EH2 1DG, and John Murray, 50 Albemarle Street, London W1X 4BD
Teachers' guides on three main topics: computation and structure; shape and size; pictorial representation and graphs leading to algebra.
Into Secondary School
*Modules – twenty modules each consisting of a set of cards for pupils and a teacher's book. The following titles have been published:
*Speed and Gradient 1
*Decimals 1
*Symmetry
*Number Patterns 1
*Angles, Courses and Bearings

Local education authority project
North West Regional Curriculum Development Project
English Materials – *Situations*. Publisher: Blackie & Sons, Bishopbriggs, Glasgow
Domestic studies materials – *Myself Now, Myself at Home* and *Myself from Birth*. Publisher: Holmes McDougall, 30 Royal Terrace, Edinburgh EH7 5AL
Social education materials – *Vocation, Consumer Education, Freedom and Responsibility, Conservation, Marriage and Homemaking, Towards Tomorrow*, and **The*

156

British. Publisher: Macmillan Education, Houndmills, Basingstoke, Hampshire RG21 2XS

Privately sponsored project
Midland Mathematics Experiment
Publisher: George Harrap & Co., 182 High Holborn, London WC1
CSE and GCE O-level courses
Examples in Modern Mathematics: Source Book
Excursions from Mathematics (Books 1 and 2)

Appendix C Relevant Schools Council and government publications

Schools Council publications

Working Papers

10. *Curriculum Development: Teachers' Groups and Contres.* HMSO, 1967.
11. *Society and the Young School Leaver: a Humanities Programme in Preparation for the Raising of the School Leaving Age.* HMSO, 1967.
14. *Mathematics for the Majority: a Programme in Mathematics for the Young School Leaver.* HMSO, 1967.
15. *Counselling in Schools: a Study of the Present Situation in England and Wales.* HMSO, 1967.
17. *Community Service and the Curriculum.* HMSO, 1968.
26. *Education through the Use of Materials: the Possible Role of School Workshops in the Education of Secondary-school Pupils.* Evans/Methuen Educational, 1969.
27. *'Cross'd with Adversity': the Education of Socially Disadvantaged Children in Secondary Schools.* Evans/Methuen Educational, 1970.
33. *Choosing a Curriculum for the Young School Leaver.* Evans/Methuen Educational, 1971.
36. *Religious Education in Secondary Schools.* Evans/Methuen Educational, 1971.
39. *Social studies 8–13.* Evans/Methuen Educational, 1971.
43. *School Resource Centres.* Evans/Methuen Educational, 1972.
51. *Social Education: an Experiment in Four Secondary Schools.* Evans/Methuen Educational, 1974.

Examinations Bulletins

21. *CSE: an Experiment in the Oral Examining of Chemistry.* Evans/Methuen Educational, 1971.

Curriculum Bulletins

1. *Mathematics in Primary Schools.* HMSO, 1965, 4th edn, 1972.
4. *Home Economics Teaching.* Evans/Methuen Educational, 1971.

Other publications

Enquiry 1: Young School Leavers. HMSO, 1968.
Humanities for the Young School Leaver: an Approach through History. Evans/Methuen Educational, 1969.
Humanities for the Young School Leaver: an Approach through Religious Education. Evans/Methuen Educational, 1969.
Out and About: a Teacher's Guide to Safety on Educational Visits. Evans/Methuen Educational, 1972.
Pterodactyls and Old Lace: Museums in Education. Evans/Methuen Educational, 1972.

Government publications

Report of Advisory Committee on Handicapped Children. *Children with Specific Reading Difficulties.* HMSO, 1972.
Slow Learners in Secondary Schools (Education Survey 15). HMSO, 1971.

Project consultative committee

Hugh Cunningham (Chairman)	Headmaster, Madeley Court School, Telford, Shropshire
Miss M. E. Aspinall	Headmistress, St Hild's Primary School, Durham
Miss H. M. Carter	Curriculum Officer, Schools Council
E. Daynes	Tutor, Course for Teachers in Special Education, Maria Grey College of Education, Twickenham, Middlesex
R. Edwards	Head of Remedial Department, Dartmouth Comprehensive School, West Bromwich
J. Gray	Headmaster, Hattersley County Comprehensive School, Hyde; now at Goyt Bank School, Stockport
Mrs J. Gregory	Remedial Teaching Service, Dudley, Worcestershire
Miss E. Hanks	Headmistress, Mount Pleasant Comprehensive School, Birmingham
C. Mowforth	Peripatetic Remedial Teacher, Berkshire (Member of Schools Council Working Party on Special Education)
R. H. Oakley	Head of Remedial Department, Pendeford High School, Wolverhampton (Member of Schools Council Working Party on Special Education)
Miss A. Rees	Schools Council Project on Curricular Needs of Slow Learning Pupils
H. G. Williams, HMI	Divisional Specialist, HM Inspectorate of Schools

159